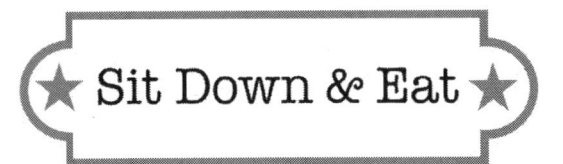

★ Sit Down & Eat ★

*To my dear family:
I can't imagine anybody with whom
I'd rather SIT DOWN & EAT every day
than all of you*

Sit Down & Eat

Fun Ideas for Making Mealtimes Memorable

By Jennifer Flanders

Prescott Publishing
Tyler, Texas

Copyright © 2017, Jennifer Flanders

Cover design, interior design, and typesetting:
Jennifer Flanders

Cover photos:
Microsoft Office Stock Photos (front)
David Flanders Photography (back)

Publisher:
Prescott Publishing
3668 Southwood Drive
Tyler, TX 75707
http://prescottpublishing.org

Sit Down & Eat: Fun Ideas for Making Mealtimes Memorable
ISBN: 978-1-938945-35-9
LCCN:

Unless otherwise noted, all Scripture references are taken from THE NEW AMERICAN STANDARD BIBLE ®, Copyright ©1960, 1962, 1963, 1968, 1971, 1972, 1973, 1975, 1977, 1995 by the Lockman Foundation. Used by permission.

The ideas and suggestions espoused in this book are not intended as a substitute for consulting with a physician. This book is intended as a reference volume only, not as a medical manual. Neither the author nor the publisher shall be liable or responsible for any loss or damage allegedly arising from any information or suggestion in this book. Mention of specific companies, organizations, or authorities in this book does not imply endorsement by the authors or publisher, nor does mention of specific companies, organizations, or authorities imply that they endorse this book, its authors, or the publisher.

- CONTENTS -

Foreword by Doug Flanders, MD xi
Introduction xiii

Section 1: A Cozy Kitchen

1. The Heart of the Home 3
2. A Place to Gather 4
3. Clean & Pretty 5
4. The Writing's on the Wall 6
5. A Place for Everything 7
6. A Well-Stocked Pantry 8
7. Containers & Canisters 9

Section 2: Table Setting

8. Choosing Sides 13
9. Fine China 14
10. Placemats 13
11. Napkin Folding 14
12. Centerpieces 16
13. Seating Assignments 18
14. Paper Plates 19

Section 3: Cooking Takes Teamwork

15. Menu Planning 23
16. Kitchen Helpers 24
17. Safety First 25
18. Life Skills Training 26
19. Divide and Conquer 27

Section 4: Giving Thanks

20. Mealtime Blessings 31
21. Taking Turns 32
22. Holding Hands 33
23. Grateful Hearts 34
24. Picky Eaters 35
25. No Complaints 36
26. Just One Bite 37

Section 5: Dinnertime Discussions

27. Pocket the Cell Phones 41
28. Sharing Stories 42
29. Low Point/ High Point 43
30. Open-Ended Questions 44
31. Current Events 45
32. Good Manners 46
33. Bible Reading 47

Section 6: Clean-Up Crew

34. Chore Assignments 51
35. Working Together 52
36. Crank Up the Music 53
37. Clean or Dirty? 54
38. What to Do with the Leftovers 55

Section 7: Holiday Happenings

39. Birthday Candles 59
40. Valentine's Day Brunch 60
41. Texas Independence Day Barbecue 61

42. Feed Me, I'm Irish! 62
43. Don't Be Fooled on April 1 63
44. Christ is Risen Indeed! 64
45. Cinco de Mayo Fiesta 65
46. Fourth of July Picnic 66
47. Trick or Treat 67
48. Thanksgiving Bounty 68
49. Christmas Morning 69

Section 8: Making the Ordinary Extra-Ordinary

50. Theme Dinners 73
51. They Call It Bella Notte 74
52. South of the Border 75
53. Chop Suey 76
54. Hawaiian Luau 77
55. Color Coded Meals 78
56. Costume Dinners 79

Section 9: Breakfast of Champions

57. Teddy Bear Toast 83
58. Egg Muffins 84
59. Fresh Fruit Smoothies 85
60. Breakfast Casserole 86
61. Homemade Granola 87
62. Ice Cream for Breakfast 88
63. Blueberry Muffins 89
64. Cooked-to-Order Pancakes 90
65. Sticky Buns 91

Section 10: Bread Baking for Beginners

66. Homemade vs. Store Bought 95
67. Garlic Bread 96
68. Cheddar Biscuits 97
69. Whole Wheat Bread 98
70. Banana Nut Bread 99

Section 11: Soup's On

71. Marvelous Minestrone 103
72. Chicken and Noodles 104
73. Taco Soup 105
74. Garlicky Lentils 106
75. Chicken Tortilla Soup 107

Section 12: Rabbit Food

76. Broccoli Cauliflower Salad 111
77. Tex-Mex Salad 112
78. All-American Potato Salad 113
79. Savor-It-Slowly Guacamole 114
80. Mama's Signature Salad 115
81. Chicken Salad 116
82. Black Bean Salad 117

Section 13: The Main Event

83. King Ranch Chicken 121
84. Cheese Enchiladas 122
85. Mama's Meatloaf 123
86. Spaghetti with Meat Sauce 124
87. Spicy Grilled Salmon 125
88. Crispy Tacos 126
89. Breaded & Baked Tilapia 127

Section 14: Crockpot Cooking

- 90. Fix It and Forget It 131
- 91. Cranberry Chicken w/ Green Beans 132
- 92. Sunday Roast w/ Carrots and Potatoes 133
- 93. Baked Apples 134
- 94. Baked Lasagna 135
- 95. Pinto Beans with Ham 136
- 96. Turkey Cheese Melts 137

Section 15: Sensational Sides

- 97. Sweet Potato Fries 141
- 98. Green Bean Casserole 142
- 99. Parmesan-Crusted Asparagus Spears 143
- 100. Spicy Beet Fries 144
- 101. Roasted Brussels Sprouts 145

Section 16: Delectable Desserts

- 102. Chocolate Delight 149
- 103. Blackberry Crumble 150
- 104. Peanut Butter Cookies 151
- 105. Rice Crispy Treats 152
- 106. No- Bake Chocolate Cookies 153

Section 17: Time-Saving Shortcuts

- 107. Perfect Pasta 157
- 108. Big Batch Cooking 158
- 109. Freezer Meals 159
- 110. How to Boil an Egg 160
- 111. Grocery Shopping 161

Afterword 163

- FOREWORD -

I never would have guessed thirty years ago, when my wife and I first got married, that one day she would be writing a cookbook. After all, her motto back then was "Who needs a dinner bell when you've got a smoke alarm?" The things that made our mealtimes most memorable in those days were the grease fires on the stove top, the black smoke billowing from our kitchen window, and the charred edges on nearly everything she set on the table.

Luckily, over the ensuing years, both her culinary skills and her presentation have improved dramatically, as you will see in the pages that follow. What's more, our children have all become excellent cooks in their own right.

Interestingly, two things that have been linked to success later in life are childhood chores and regular meals with the family. So cooking and cleaning together is actually beneficial long after the meal is digested and forgotten. It is our hope that the helpful hints you'll find in this book will benefit not only you and your children, but many generations to come!

Eat up, and God bless!
- Doug Flanders, MD

- INTRODUCTION -

In this age of fast food restaurants, cram-packed schedules, and segmented families who must eat on the go as they hurry off in different directions every night of the week, the family dinner hour is becoming a relic of the past.

If you can't remember when you last gathered around the family table for a leisurely, home-cooked meal with every member present and engaged in a single conversation (no cell phones or surreptitious texting allowed!), then you've come to the right place.

Regular family meals offer the kind of body and soul nourishing fare on which both children and parents thrive, but it doesn't happen by accident. If you want your kids to grow up with positive memories of regularly shared mealtimes, you must be intentional about creating them.

That's where this book can help—so tuck in. Whether you're interested in preparing special dishes, planning themed dinners, establishing new family traditions, or engaging your children in meaningful conversations, in the pages that follow, you'll find a veritable smorgasbord of fun ideas for making mealtimes memorable.

Section 1

A Cozy Kitchen

Section 1: A Cozy Kitchen

-1-
The Heart of a Home

Ever wonder why the kitchen is known as "the heart of the home?"

Maybe it's because the kitchen is so conveniently located. In every house I've ever lived in, the kitchen has been the first room we enter when we come home and the last room we pass through when we leave.

So much of life happens right in the kitchen. Need a drink? Go to the kitchen. Want a snack? Go to the kitchen. Need to find Mom? Check in the kitchen. ☺

The kitchen is where we store groceries, cook food, plan menus, wash dishes, and sweep crumbs. It's where we gather around the table to share meals, do homework, play games, work puzzles, make crafts, and entertain company. As homeschoolers, we even take spelling tests, write essays, do science experiments, and learn important lessons about home economics in the kitchen.

Just as the heart is responsible for pumping vital nutrients to every part of the body, the kitchen serves as sort of a Grand Central Station for getting nourishment to every member of the family. So let's do our best to keep it clean, fresh, and functioning efficiently!

-2-
A Place to Gather

I never saw the movie *Field of Dreams*, but I'm familiar with the film's most famous line: "If you build it, they will come."

Something similar could be said about homemade cuisine: "If you cook it, they will come." There's nothing like delectable smells wafting from the kitchen to draw a family together. Who can resist the smell of freshly baked bread, savory stew, or chocolate chip cookies all melty-warm from the oven?

Hunger may bring folks to the kitchen, but comfort and community will keep them there, so do what you can to make room for as many around your table as possible.

As our family grew, we had to forgo chairs in favor of sturdy benches that would accommodate more little bottoms in less space. Having counter stools around an island and side chairs in the den allows us to easily pull in extra seating when we have guests. Even if some of us end up balancing our plates on our laps, it's nice to eat and fellowship together as a group as often as possible, and the kitchen is the prime place for that to happen!

Section 1: A Cozy Kitchen

-3-
Clean & Pretty

Just as an unmade bed makes the whole bedroom look messy, a grungy kitchen can make the entire house seem dirty. Maintaining a perfectly spotless kitchen is probably not a very practical goal—especially when there are little children (or a lot of big children) living in the house—but the opposite extreme is completely unacceptable.

To keep a kitchen clean, just be faithful about completing these four basic chores after every meal or snack:

- DO THE DISHES: Wash and dry them immediately or load them in a dishwasher—no daily mound of dirty dinnerware in the kitchen sink!
- PUT AWAY FOOD: Place leftovers in the fridge and return ingredients used in preparing the meal to the pantry—bonus points for cleaning up as you go.
- CLEAN OFF SURFACES: Wipe down counters and tabletops—no drippy-drips or sticky fingerprints.
- SWEEP UP CRUMBS: You don't have to move out all the chairs and mop after every meal, but do grab a dustpan, spot check the floor, and wipe up any spills.

To make a kitchen pretty, simply add tasteful artwork to the walls (pun intended), cheery curtains at the windows, and an arrangement of fresh fruit or cut flowers on the table.

-4-
The Writing's on the Wall

I love the look of Bible verses or pithy quotes painted directly on the wall in a beautiful script—and the kitchen provides a perfect canvas to do this. One of the homes we've lived in had a huge triple window behind the dining table, so I painted 1 Corinthians 10:31 in an Old English font above it:

"Whether then you eat or drink or whatever you do, do all for the glory of God."

It was a long expanse of wall, so I had plenty of room to spell out the words in a single line of lettering. But here's a few shorter verses that would be great in smaller spaces:

- *"Taste and see that the Lord is good." (Psalm 34:8)*
- *"Give us this day our daily bread." (Luke 11:3)*
- *"Give thanks to the Lord, for He is good." (Psalm 106:1)*
- *"Man shall not live by bread alone." (Matthew 4:4)*
- *"As for me and my house, we shall serve the Lord." (Joshua 24:15)*

Penmanship too shaky for hand lettering? No worries. Vinyl transfers are now available that give you the same great look without the hassle. And you can customize all the details to suit your own particular style.

Section 1: A Cozy Kitchen

-5-
A Place for Everything

Does the counter in your kitchen become a catchall for clutter? Schoolbooks, art projects, junk mail—do these tend to gather (and multiply) on your table or bar? Those familiar old words Mom used to quote are especially helpful here: *A place for everything and everything in place.* Next time your kitchen counters are their messiest, take stock of the things that are stacked there and brainstorm a better home for each misplaced category:

- If you find mail scattered there, invest in a pretty file or wall pocket for the kitchen, with separate slots for incoming mail, bills, and outgoing letters. Drop junk mail in the trash immediately (or stop it at the source by calling 1-800-5-OPT-OUT).

- Schoolbooks stacked by the sink? Repurpose a hutch or sideboard into shelves where kids can stash their school supplies when not in use.

- If your child's toys or books migrate to the kitchen, gather them into a wicker basket and insist that the basket is checked and items put away before meals.

- If dirty dishes seem to be multiplying on your kitchen counters, get in the habit of cleaning up quickly after every meal. Instate a new rule: anyone who eats a between-meal snack must clean up again afterwards.

-6-
A Well-Stocked Pantry

Having a well-provisioned pantry has always been a boon to families who want to eat hearty meals at home. That fact hasn't changed, although the foods that commonly line our shelves today bear little resemblance to the staples found in your great-grandma's kitchen.

Where the pioneers had salt pork, smoked venison, sweet cream butter, potatoes, onions, corn meal, and molasses, we have individually packaged snack foods and hamburger helper. Unfortunately, grab-n-go convenience foods are not always the most healthful choices. Find a few good-for-you recipes that can be made quickly and try to keep the ingredients on hand for those dishes at all times. Taco soup (p. 105), chicken noodle soup (p. 104) and garlicky lentils (p. 106) are some of my go-to meals that fit this description.

Other long-lasting staples you'll find stashed in my pantry include:

- Dried beans: black, pinto, split peas, lentils
- Grains: oats, wild rice, barley, quinoa
- Pasta: egg noodles, macaroni, spaghetti
- Herbs & spices: salt, pepper, garlic, oregano
- Canned goods: tomato paste, chicken, fruit
- Baking goods: flour, sugar, baking soda, yeast

Section 1: A Cozy Kitchen

-7-
Containers & Canisters

When I was first setting up house, I spotted some toffee peanuts at Sam's that came packaged in a clear, square, reusable container. A row of four fit perfectly in the wire shelving that hung on my pantry door at the time, so I stocked up. I bought sixteen or twenty of them and—once we'd polished off the peanuts and removed the labels—used them to store pasta, rice, beans, goldfish, and granola.

I love the tidy, uniform look of a well-organized pantry, and those matching "freebie" canisters made mine look neat as a pin. Other advantages to using airtight containers for storing snacks and staples include:

- *Freshness:* keeps crisp things crisp & soft things soft
- *Visibility:* shows at a glance when supplies are low
- *Protection:* protects against bugs & other pests

My repurposed canisters were durable and stayed with us for many years (but I'm pretty sure the 20 pounds I gained from eating all those toffee peanuts stayed even longer). When the time finally came to replace them, I invested in an expanded set of Tupperware Modular Mates.® They were pricier than my peanut jars, but easier on my hips! ☺

Section 2

Table Setting

Section 2: Table Setting

-8-
Choosing Sides

Do you ever have trouble remembering which utensil goes on which side when setting the table? I used to, until I learned this little trick to remind me:

- The words F-O-R-K and L-E-F-T have four letters, so forks go on the left.
- K-N-I-F-E and S-P-O-O-N both have five letters, just like R-I-G-H-T, so those utensils go on the right.

The napkin goes on the left, to keep the fork from getting lonely—unless, of course, you fold it fancy (see chapter 11), in which case it can take center stage atop the plate.

These rules are sufficient for most of the plain-Jane meals our family eats at home. If you're really putting on the Ritz, you should remember that soup spoons stay on the right with teaspoons, while salad forks and seafood forks keep the dinner fork company on the left. The butter knife goes on the bread plate about 10 o'clock to the dinner plate; water glasses or tea glasses are placed at the tip of the knife.

Oh, and be sure to place any fork or spoon intended for dessert horizontally above your plate. You wouldn't want it getting dirty before the cake and ice cream is served!

Sit Down & Eat

-9-
Fine China

Many couples today never even bother picking a formal china pattern, but back when my husband and I got married, fine china was considered a central part of one's bridal registry.

We chose "Juliet," a Royal Dalton pattern of ivory porcelain with a delicate border of pink roses and pale blue and gold scrollwork. I still think it's the prettiest china I've ever seen.

As providence would have it, our family quickly outgrew the five or six place settings we received as wedding gifts, and so that beautiful dinnerware eventually got relegated to a locked china closet, still visible but seldom used.

A few years ago, however, my husband surprised me by completing our set for Christmas, so now I've moved it all to a kitchen shelf where it is more easily accessible.

Do you have fine china or fancy dinnerware that you only get out on special occasions (if *then*)? I'd encourage you to use it more often than that.

A beautifully set table can make any day seem special, so put your pretty things within easy reach, then *reach for them* more often and let your family know that they're special enough to eat off the "company" plates.

Section 2: Table Setting

-10-
Placemats

My mother is the placemat queen. She has a collection of beautiful, quilted mats which she color-coordinates with seasonal dishes, centerpieces, and napkin rings all year long. Her table is always set and ready for company, which makes her kitchen look especially pretty and inviting.

As much as I admire my mother's housekeeping habits, I do not own many quilted placemats of my own. However, I do have some laminated copies of world maps, US presidents, Bible verses, prayer guides, periodic tables, and other such homeschool helps that occasionally get pressed into service as placemats around our dinner table.

One homeschooling family I know slides such charts and diagrams under a clear vinyl tablecloth. That way, they can use dinnertime to review memory work and still get things cleaned up quickly and easily after the meal is over.

Another option I often employed when our children were younger was to put them to work creating their own placemats out of large pieces of construction paper. They were allowed to decorate them any way they liked. This practice made for lots of bright and colorful place settings, while also keeping my little ones occupied and within my line of vision as I prepared dinner. A win-win, for sure!

Sit Down & Eat

-11-
Napkin Folding

Immediately following 9-11, the bottom dropped out of the travel market, and our family was able to take a fabulous 8-day Caribbean cruise for cents on the dollar. Of the many onboard activities offered during our days at sea, my favorite was a class in napkin folding. Napkin art is like origami, only it uses fabric squares instead of paper.

Whether you stand an accordion-folded fan in a napkin ring or wine glass or you choose a more intricate design like this slipper, folded napkins can really dress up a dinner table:

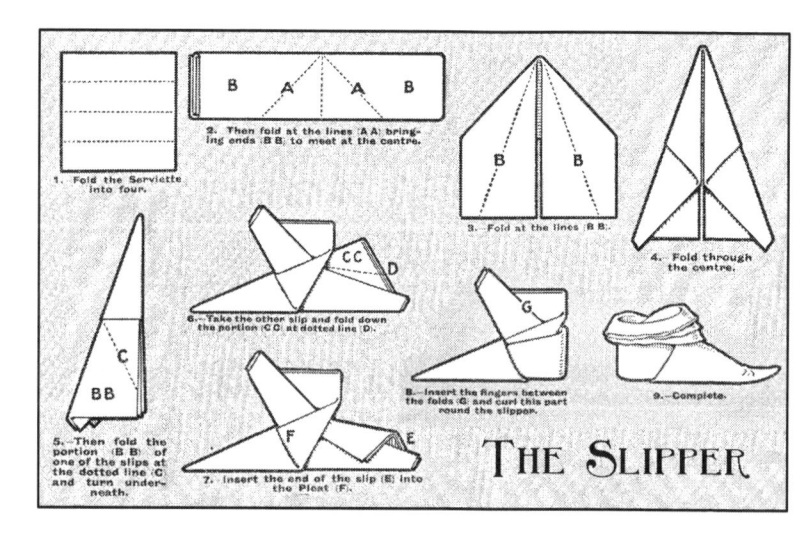

Section 2: Table Setting

-12-
Centerpieces

There's nothing that spruces up a table setting faster than a pretty centerpiece. Whether you're serving a meal buffet-style or seating guests for a formal dinner, a pretty arrangement in the middle of the table makes everything look more festive.

Tall crystal vases of fresh flowers and tiered serving trays are fine for a buffet table, but anytime I decorate a table where people will be sitting, I go for shorter arrangements that won't obstruct their line of vision during dinnertime conversations. Here are a few of my favorite low-profile centerpiece ideas:

- votive candles set among creeping vines of ivy
- a line of mason jars filled with wild flowers
- a wooden tray full of fresh fruit or potted succulents
- a grouping of autumn pumpkins, gourds & pine cones
- a row of small wrapped gifts set among sprigs of holly

-13-
Seating Assignments

When one has a family as large as ours, assigned seats can make mealtimes more peaceful. Despite the fact that in all Norman Rockwall's idyllic paintings, the father occupies the seat of honor at the head of the table, my husband prefers to sit on the center of one side, right in the middle of the action.

I always sit across from him, that way, we are both closer to the children and to the food we're attempting to serve to their plates. The youngest ones sit on my right and left. The next youngest next to Dad, and the older ones staggered down the table from there, where they can easily join in on the conversation and lend a hand as needed in refilling plates or water glasses. We have two left-handers in the family, who get relegated to the ends of the table, to cut down on knocking elbows.

When we had eleven children living at home, our kitchen table was ten feet long and each child occupied an assigned seat. (I made seating charts not just for daily mealtimes, but for riding in our van and sitting in the den for nightly story time, as well.) This practice helped keep bickering about *who sat where last* at bay. Now that we're down to only seven children at home (three of whom often miss dinner), our table is smaller and the charts aren't nearly as important.

Section 2: Table Setting

-14-
Paper Plates

Lest all this talk about fine china and fancy centerpieces should make some mother feel like she isn't doing enough in the kitchen, let me hurry to say that I definitely believe there is a time and place for paper plates and quick, efficient meals.

For us, that time is normally in the middle of a school day. When lunchtime rolls around, we take a break from our lessons long enough to grab something fast and easy to eat and clean up.

Sandwiches served on a paper plate—or, better yet, *a paper towel*—with a side of raw fruit or veggies, and we're ready to hit the books again in about fifteen minutes flat.

We also use a lot of paper plates during the summer months for picnic dinners at the neighborhood pool. I like it best when there's no leftovers. That way, clean-up can be finished in a flash.

When we return home an hour later, everyone is squeaky fresh from our evening swim. So we all change straight into our pajamas, ready to read story time then go to bed.

Section 3

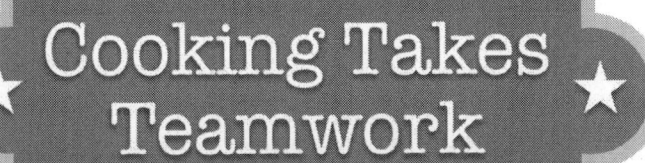

Cooking Takes Teamwork

Section 3: Cooking Takes Teamwork

-15-
Menu Planning

Planning out meals ahead of time really pays off. Whether you make your menu a week at a time or plan out a whole month's worth of meals (or you decide what you're going to serve for dinner in the morning, instead of waiting until five minutes before Dad is due home from work to start thinking about it), both your hungry family and your food budget will appreciate your forethought.

Having a good game plan will cut down on unplanned meals out, unnecessary fast food purchases, and unexpected 11th hour runs to the grocery store. All that translates into more time to spend at home with your family.

If you really want to keep them happy, enlist their help in the decision making process. Compile a list of your family's favorite meals and special requests for breakfast, lunch, and dinner, then work those dishes into your menu and add the necessary ingredients to your shopping list.

Your menu needn't be set in stone. It's possible to plan ahead and still be flexible. If you're hesitant to decide on Monday what you'll eat for dinner on Friday, then make a list of 5-7 meals, buy the groceries required to make them, and wait until the day dawns to pick which you'll eat when.

-16-
Kitchen Helpers

Have you ever noticed that, sometimes, the children most eager to help are the ones least capable of doing so? Often it takes two or three times as long to accomplish a task *with helpers* than without.

That said, you'll want to be careful not to quench this early enthusiasm! If you can find ways to put your happy volunteers to work while they're little, they will continue to be cheerful helpers, even when they're big.

Plus, they'll learn the joy of making a meaningful contribution and taking pride in a job well-done.

Since my youngest helpers usually want to do whatever job they see me doing, I've found it helpful to invest in extra potato peelers, melon scoops, and paring knives. This allows them to join in without slowing progress, despite their inexperience.

It doesn't matter that I can skin five carrots in the time it takes them to peel one—since I have four or five vegetable peelers, we can all work together and get the job done that much faster!

Section 3: Cooking Takes Teamwork

-17-
Safety First

Anytime you have children in the kitchen, safety is a concern. This is true whether little ones are "helping" or not. In my mind, burns are a much bigger threat than cuts, so I make certain pan handles are turned toward the back of the stove where little ones can't reach them. Also, I have others stand back when I'm pouring boiling water off pasta, releasing steam on my pressure cooker, or opening the lid to a hot gas grill.

When it comes to cutting, chopping, slicing, and dicing, sharp tools are safer than dull ones, but younger children will still need close supervision when lending a hand. Here's a run down for the ages we let children do certain tasks in food preparation:

- Ages 2-4: tear lettuce, de-stem grapes, rinse fruits and veggies, scoop melon balls, make toast
- Ages 5-7: peel carrots or potatoes, use garlic mincer or lemon juicer, dice avocados with a dinner knife
- Ages 8-10: fry or scramble eggs, slice tomatoes with a sharp knife, bake cookies or brownies
- Ages 11-13: bake bread, operate mixer, blender, or food processor, prepare simple meals and snacks
- Age 14 and up: plan menus, make salads, sides, main dishes, and desserts with little or no assistance

-18-
Life-Skill Training

By teaching your children how to cook before they leave home, you will give them a huge leg up in life. And the younger they are when they start learning, the better.

My little sister loved to help in the kitchen when we were growing up. Anytime Mom was cooking, you could count on Kimberly to be right there at her side. Consequently, my sister has always been an accomplished cook and—what's more—seems to truly enjoy the process.

I was far more likely to follow my father around as a child, asking questions and watching him fix things. So while Kimberly could prepare a five-course meal when she married, I could barely boil water. My poor husband and children suffered for years while I tried to play catch-up in the kitchen.

On the bright side, hanging out with Dad definitely had its perks. I am fully capable of setting a toilet or switching out a light fixture, and my sister learned how to shingle a roof before she left home. But my sweet mother was such an excellent cook, I've always wished I'd taken a little more interest in learning all her culinary tips and tricks while we were living under the same roof.

Section 3: Cooking Takes Teamwork

-19-
Divide and Conquer

A wise sage once observed, "Many hands make light labor." This truism is particularly good to remember when trying to get dinner on the table.

With twelve children to feed and lots of their neighborhood friends who regularly joined us for dinner, our kitchen often resembled a mess hall.

To speed up the preparation process, we put everybody to work—including guests!

- one child sets the table
- another fills the water pitchers and puts ice in glasses
- one butters and toasts the bread
- another makes the salad
- Mom works on the main course
- another child readies fresh fruit or dessert
- extra hands help clean up as we go

And the youngest calls everyone not already in the kitchen to dinner just as soon as it's time to eat!

Section 4

Giving Thanks

Section 4: Giving Thanks

-20-
Mealtime Blessings

My husband says the same simple prayer before every meal. It seldom varies: *"God, thank you for this food. Help it bless and nourish our bodies. In Jesus' name I pray, Amen."* There's little chance the food will grow cold if Doug's the one saying grace! His prayers are short, sweet, and to the point—but that doesn't mean they aren't heartfelt.

Pausing before a meal long enough to pray over the food is a good way to acknowledge the God from whose hand we receive all of life's blessings. Some may protest, "But I'm the one who worked the job and earned the money and bought the groceries and cooked the food—why thank God for something I did myself?"

Because God is the one who provided the job and gave you the brains and the health and the strength to keep it. He's the one who made the sun and sent the rain and caused the crops to grow so there'd be something to buy when you shopped for groceries. God is the one who let you live in a country where the currency is stable and food is available and you're free to purchase what you like. And He is the one who gave you a home to live in and a kitchen to cook in and a family to share the meal with.

When we bow our heads before we eat, we're thanking God for much, much more than our food—and He knows it.

Sit Down & Eat

-21-
Taking Turns

Asking God to bless the food before we eat is a simple tradition that helps keep us all mindful of the One from whence "our daily bread" comes.

In my husband's family, they always took turns saying grace before every meal: Father would pray before breakfast, Mother at lunch, brother at dinner, then sister at breakfast the following day.

They'd take turns by age, going from oldest to youngest, until each person had had a chance to thank God for a meal, then they'd begin all over and do it again.

We've followed this same pattern with our own children, only it takes us nearly a week to get through us all!

We're hopeful that the practice will do the following three things for our children:

1. Develop their sense of gratitude for all of God's bountiful blessings
2. Build their confidence in what an easy matter it is to pray or converse with God
3. Help them from a young age to feel comfortable speaking in front of a crowd

Section 4: Giving Thanks

-22-
Holding Hands

Our family joins hands during mealtime prayers for two very practical reasons (besides the fact that doing so helps build our immune systems):

First, linking hands provides a wordless way to let people at the far ends of the table know that it is time to say grace.

Little children, especially, are much more apt to keep quiet for the prayer (and to resist any compelling urges to sneak bites of food from their own plate or that of their neighbor) when their potentially offending fingers are thus occupied while heads are bowed and eyes are closed.

Just as importantly, hand holding benefits those who might have a hard time hearing a timidly spoken "Amen."

A couple of quick hand squeezes at the conclusion of the prayer keeps everyone at the dinner table in perfect sync.

That's important when you have a couple of dozen people all dining together, like we do every weekend when most of our children and all of our grandsons join us for lunch at Luby's Cafeteria. (They let kids eat free on Saturdays—one free child's meal per adult meal purchased—a great deal for the likes of us!)

Sit Down & Eat

-23-
Grateful Hearts

Mealtimes provide an excellent opportunity to express gratitude, not only to our Heavenly Father through prayer, but also to the sweet souls who so faithfully prepare our food.

The best way to establish this habit, which is really just a sign of (what should be) common courtesy, is by training children to thank their mother (or whoever else may have done the cooking) after each and every meal at home.

- "Thanks for dinner, Mom. It was delicious."
- "Thank you, Dad. I really enjoyed that meal."
- "Thank you, Grandma. You cook great!"
- "That was very filling, Mother. Thanks!"
- "Thanks, Daddy. I appreciate your hard work."
- "Thank you, Mom. What can I do to help clean up?"
- "Thanks, Nana. That was my favorite!"
- "Thank you, Mother. You're the best."

You get the idea. Is that too much to ask? If you'll instill this habit in your children at home, it will naturally follow them into other social settings, as well, where such refined manners will set them worlds apart from their peers and serve them well throughout their lives.

Section 4: Giving Thanks

-24-
Picky Eaters

On the opposite end of the good manners scale from sincere gratitude is excessive pickiness. If this describes your child, you'll want to do what you can to break it, albeit gently, without turning the dinner hour into WWIII.

Rather than becoming some sort of short order cook or catering to your child's every whim, serve him the same varied, healthful meals you put before the rest of the family, but always include at least one side dish you know he will gladly eat.

For several of my children, that side dish was salad. For others, it was bread or mashed potatoes.

Encourage them to try new things (see p. 37), but allow them to "tank up" on that one staple item if nothing else suits their fancy.

Their tastes will mature as they grow, and they'll eventually expand their list of favored foods if you can avoid making mealtimes a battleground. Some of my pickiest eaters as children became my easiest-to-please eaters as adults, while still remaining very health conscious in their personal food choices.

-25-
No Complaints

A corollary to dealing with picky eaters of all ages is to outlaw complaints about what is served.

It is disheartening for any cook who has labored long over a meal to have to listen to constant belly-aching from those for whom it was intended:

- "I don't like _____."
- "Why can't we eat _____ instead?"
- "I hate it when we have _____."
- "Do I *have* to eat _____?"
- "Why do you always have to make _____?"
- "I've lost my appetite."

Comments like these are completely unacceptable and should be banned from dinnertime conversations.

Don't let your child voice such negativism at home, or he will be just as ungrateful and disrespectful to his hosts and hostesses when he is in other people's homes.

And that would be a real shame.

Section 4: Giving Thanks

-26-
Just One Bite

Growing up, I had a friend whose mom saved whatever he refused to eat at one meal and served it the next.

I don't know about you, but I doubt I'd recall my childhood very fondly if I'd routinely had the same bowl of soggy cereal set before me several meals running. I'm grateful my mother chose a different tack. Anytime I was reluctant to eat something, she'd encourage me to try "just one bite." Who knows? Maybe I'd like it. If not, she didn't make me eat it. There were plenty of other options on the table, and if nothing there appealed to me, there'd be another meal a few hours later—no grazing on junk food in the interim.

Thanks to her efforts, I learned to like a wide variety of healthful foods from a young age, although it was not until I was an adult that I finally developed a fondness for green beans. Now they're my favorite, but I had a hard time even swallowing "just one bite" as a child. I'd gag every time.

I'm so glad my parents took such a balanced approach to training my taste buds. They didn't reward finicky-ness by catering to my every culinary whim, but neither did they try to break me of personal preferences by making battles over diet a hill on which to die. They suspected I would eventually come around—and they were right.

Section 5

Dinnertime Discussions

Section 5: Dinnertime Discussions

-27-
Pocket the Cell Phones

I once saw an ad for a product called the "Power-Down Peppermill." One twist and every electronic devise within 30 feet instantaneously shut off. Since the nifty little gadget actually ground pepper whenever it was twisted, as well, no one ever suspected Mom was behind the mysterious power outage.

I think it was a spoof ad, but if anybody ever came up with such an invention, I imagine it would make a fortune. Cell phones and social media enable us to connect with people on the other side of the planet, but they often prevent our connecting with people on the other side of the table.

Modern day parents are just as likely to offend in this area as their teen and adolescent children. How many times I've observed families dining out together where every person at the table was absorbedly fiddling with something on their phone. No conversation. No eye contact. Everybody was in their own little world: Mom, Dad, teens and tweens.

Parents, set the example. Pocket your cell phones during family meals. Require your children and guests to do the same. The digital world will still be waiting when you're done; dinnertime should be used to connect and fellowship with the family and friends who are right in front of us.

Sit Down & Eat

-28-
Sharing Stories

Sometimes my husband is too busy to call home during the workday, despite the fact there are things he'd like to tell me. So he does the next best thing; he keeps a running list of notes:

- Interesting things that happened
- Bits of news he read
- People or places he saw
- Funny things that were said

He writes down just enough on each topic to jog his memory once we're together again, so he won't forget.

Mealtime is the perfect place to share such stories. We all love hearing about one another's days this way. With a family as large as ours, it's easy to get several table time conversations going at once, but it works much better when one person talks at a time, and everybody else listens.

By having a single conversation over the dinner table, children (and adults) learn to listen and be respectful of one another. They get to practice important give-and-take conversational skills like taking turns and sharing attention. And they learn things they mightn't know if they did all the talking themselves. All good stuff, don't you think?

Section 5: Dinnertime Discussions

-29-
Low Point/ High Point

What of family members who don't keep a running list of conversation fodder in their front pockets? How do you draw reluctant speakers into the conversation?

One of the easiest ways we've found is by playing a game we call "Low Point/ High Point." We got started on this years ago during one of our road trips, and now it is a family tradition.

On the last day of our vacation, usually as we're driving toward home, Dad will call "Low Point/ High Point," then everybody will take turns telling what their favorite and least favorite memories were from our trip.

We go in order, youngest to oldest, and it is always interesting to hear what everyone has to say. Sometimes one person's favorite activity was another's least favorite, and vice versa. Sometimes the kids remember things that, by the end of the vacation, I've already forgotten we even did.

The same game works great for dinnertime, too. Take turns telling about the low and high points of your day that day. Listen up, and you may be surprised by what you hear!

Sit Down & Eat

-30-
Open-Ended Questions

If you really want to get your family members talking, you'll have to learn the art of asking open-ended questions. These are questions that cannot be answered with simple "yes" or "no" answers, but require a little more thought and details.

If you want to know this:	Ask it this way instead:
"Did you have a nice day?"	"What was the most interesting thing that happened to you today?"
"Did you finish your homework?"	"Which of your classes have assignments due soon?"
"Do you have plans this weekend?"	"What does your weekend schedule look like?"
"Are you hungry?"	"What would you like to eat for dinner tonight?"
"Did you talk to your boss today?"	"What did your boss say when you told him about your new idea?"
"Do you want to see a movie tonight?"	"What's your all-time favorite movie and why?"

Section 5: Dinnertime Discussions

-31-
Current Events

The family dinner hour is the perfect time to discuss local, national, and global news and current events.

Since our family does not own a television, the children and I are often blissfully unaware of the stories broadcast on network news. This is fine by us, as much of what passes for news on mainstream channels has little bearing on our lives and is presented with an intolerably liberal bias, anyway.

We prefer to get our news from sources that share our foundational beliefs and have proven themselves reliable. Two of the sources we turn to with the most regularity are Dad and WORLD magazine.

My husband will often bring news home from the hospital and brief us on current events over dinner. Or I will dog-ear articles in WORLD magazine to read aloud at mealtime and talk about with the children, or I'll star the most important new stories for the older kids to read independently, jotting down questions in the margins for us all to discuss once they finish reading.

That's assuming I see the magazine first. If one of the kids brings in the mail, I may not get my hands on it until they've already passed it around. ☺

-32-
Good Manners

When carrying on discussions at the dinner table, it is important that everybody practices good manners.

The list of habits we want to foster and encourage includes the following rules of civility:

- No talking with food in your mouth
- No wolfing your food just because you have something to say
- No monopolizing the conversation
- Give others a chance to speak
- Eat as quietly as possible so that others can hear what is being said
- Only one speaker allowed at a time
- Avoid topics that may cause a loss of appetite

Full disclosure: That last point is seldom followed in our house, unless we have company (and even then we sometimes forget).

When your husband or father is an articulate physician who spends his days in an operating room, you get used to—and learn to enjoy—eating while listening to fairly graphic descriptions of all manner of practices and procedures that might turn a weaker stomach.

Section 5: Dinnertime Discussions

-33-
Bible Reading

Family meals provide a great opportunity for Bible reading, too. Once everybody is seated at the breakfast table, I'll often read a Psalm or Proverb aloud to the children before beginning on my own food.

They wake up hungry after sleeping all night, so they're usually motivated to eat. While their mouths are full of food, I can usually finish a chapter or two without interruption.

Once I'm done, I eat my food while they take turns telling what they think the verses I read mean and how they can apply those Biblical truths to their lives.

I like conducting morning devotions this way. It reminds me of that charge God gave the Israelites in Deuteronomy:

> *"Therefore shall ye lay up these my words in your heart and in your soul, and bind them for a sign upon your hand, that they may be as frontlets between your eyes. And ye shall teach them your children, speaking of them when thou sittest in thine house, and when thou walkest by the way, when thou liest down, and when thou risest up."*

- Deuteronomy 11:18-19

Section 6

Clean-Up Crew

Section 6: Clean-Up Crew

-34-
Chore Assignments

When it comes to kitchen clean-up, we assign chores to our children, as do many parents. What is different about how we do it is the length of our rotation schedule.

We switch chores not daily or weekly or monthly, but once a year. That means for a full twelve months, one child is in charge of emptying the dishwasher every day, another's in charge of loading it, one's in charge of clearing the table, one's in charge of wiping off the counters, another's in charge of sweeping the floor, and so on.

There are several advantages to having a child take charge of one chore for an entire year. First, it cuts out arguments. We never hear them bickering, "I washed dishes last night, tonight it's your turn." Everybody knows who has what chore, and they don't try to worm out of them.

Second, it inspires proficiency. Knowing they'll be doing the same chore all year long motivates them to learn to do it in the most thorough (so they won't be called back) and time-efficient way possible. By the end of the year, they are experts at their tasks.

And third, by the time they leave our home, they've learned to do well everything it takes to maintain a clean kitchen.

-35-
Working Together

Chores are more bearable when everybody works together. Kids are less inclined to feel like Cinderella when parents and siblings are working right beside them.

That's why I usually stay in the kitchen during clean up, putting away food or doing some preliminary prep work for the next meal. If there's an especially large stack of dirty dishes in the sink—if we've had company over for dinner or made a bigger mess than usual cooking—I'll often pitch in and help with that chore, as well.

If a younger child is in charge of loading dishes (or if we've switched chores so recently that the loader hasn't gotten very fast at loading yet), it can be easy to feel overwhelmed by the magnitude of the mess. In those cases, I'll rinse the dishes while my child loads or vice versa.

Give them a few months, though, and they'll be handling the task like an old pro. By then, they're usually finished before I can get all the food put away, and they take such pride in the obvious progress they make. Skill building such as this is a great source of self-confidence, which is why studies show that the most successful people in the business world are those who were required to do chores as children.

Section 6: Clean-Up Crew

-36-
Crank Up the Music

We've found that one of the best ways to keep our workers from dragging their feet is to put on some lively music during clean-up time. I have a great collection of 50s tunes we use for just that purpose.

My favorite is a song called "Yakety Yak" by The Coasters, because the lyrics (via *http://www.oldielyrics.com/lyrics/the_coasters/yakety_yak.html*) are so fitting:

> *Take out the papers and the trash*
> *Or you don't get no spendin' cash*
> *If you don't scrub that kitchen floor*
> *You ain't gonna rock and roll no more*
> *Yakety yak (Don't talk back)*
>
> *Just finish cleanin' up your room*
> *Let's see the dust fly with that broom*
> *Get all that garbage out of sight*
> *Or you don't go out Friday night*
> *Yakety yak (Don't talk back)*
>
> *Now you just grab your coat and hat*
> *And get yourself to the laundry mat,*
> *And when you're finished doing that,*
> *Then feed the dog and put out the cat.*
> *Yakety yak (Don't talk back)*

-37-
Clean or Dirty?

Want a quick way to tell whether the dishes in your dishwasher are clean or dirty?

If the interior of your dishwasher is stainless steel, you can use a dry erase marker to prominently write the word "Dirty" on the inside of your dishwasher door as soon you've finished unloading (test first):

DIRTY

The word will stay there until you run your washer again, at which point it will be rinsed off. If you open the washer and see the word dirty, you'll know it's safe to keep loading. If you open it up and the word is gone, you'll know the dishes inside are squeaky clean and ready to be emptied.

No more soiling clean dishes by loading dirty ones on top of them, or putting away half a load of dirty dishes before realizing the dishwasher hasn't run!

For dishwashers without a stainless interior, try filling the detergent dispenser as soon as each load is emptied. That way, if you see a full dispenser snapped shut, you know the dishes are still dirty. If it's open and empty, they're clean.

Section 6: Clean-Up Crew

-38-
What to Do with the Leftovers

I once saw a bogus advertisement for Tupperware that said it was "for people who want to throw out their leftovers some other day of the week." And, truly, if you don't anticipate reusing the scraps of food you are squirreling away in the far recesses of your refrigerator, it would make much better sense to toss it before it grows mold and starts to smell.

Fortunately, those aren't our only two choices. My husband has long maintained that spaghetti *tastes better* the second day it is served, and for (almost) everything else, I've found creative ways to use the food we don't finish the first time:

- Freeze leftover fruit salad to be used in smoothies
- Freeze those last few bites of vegetable side dishes to be added later to soups or stews
- Pinto beans can be mashed and refried for burritos
- Turn leftover casseroles into soup by adding beef, chicken, or vegetable stock
- Chop leftover spinach or broccoli to use in a quiche
- Spoon leftover pudding or Jello into popsicle molds
- Toast leftover garlic bread slices until they're crispy enough for bruschetta or soup/salad croutons

Section 7

Holiday Happenings

Section 7: Holiday Happenings

-39-
Birthday Candles

Our birthday celebrations have evolved a lot over the years. When we had only a couple of kids, we went all-out for parties, inviting friends, cooking food, playing games, and even making costumes for the big event.

Now that we have so many, most of our birthdays are family affairs. Granted, we usually have more people in attendance now than we ever did at those early bashes, but the planning is not nearly as complicated.

The birthday child always gets to pick what/where we eat. Sometimes that involves Mom cooking a favorite meal. More often than not, it means all of us going to a restaurant of the honoree's choosing.

Some of our kids love cake, so I try to bake their favorite for the occasion. Others don't like cake at all, so I've also been known to put birthday candles in blueberry muffins, blackberry cobbler, banana pudding, fudge brownies, plain bagels, chicken pot pie, and once even a lasagna.

The lasagna was a big mistake, mainly because the child whom we were celebrating at the time really did like cake; she didn't get one because I was out of sugar at the time. In retrospect, I should have made a run to the grocery store. She's never let me live that disappointing birthday down!☺

Sit Down & Eat

-40-
Valentine's Day Brunch

With twelve kids, we'd be throwing a birthday party every time we turned around. I love parties, but don't feel right hitting our friends up for gifts on a near-monthly basis, so we find other things to celebrate with them instead.

One of my favorite traditions has been hosting our Annual Mother-Daughter Valentine Brunch, which we've done for about 20 years now. In the beginning, I did all the cooking for the brunch and everybody just visited during the party while balancing their plates on their knees. Before long, though, a few moms started offering to bring a dish to the brunch and a few of the girls began bringing their flutes and violins along to play for us while we ate.

Now, everyone brings food to share. We've enjoyed homemade quiche, sausage balls, coffee cake, heart-shaped sugar cookies, and even strawberry soup. Delicious! And all the girls come prepared to share their talents, as well. Several still play beautiful music on our piano or on instruments toted from home. Others read poetry they've written, quote passages they've memorized, show off artwork they've drawn or painted, model a dress they've sewn, or pass around pot holders they've woven or scarves they've knitted. We have lots of variety every year, and the daughters seem to enjoy the event as much as the moms do.

Section 7: Holiday Happenings

-41-
Texas Independence Day Barbecue

Texans typically take a lot of pride in their heritage. That's understandable, because Texas is a great state (in my not-too-humble opinion).

Texans celebrate their independence from Mexico annually on March 2. It's a good time to "Remember the Alamo!" "Remember Goliad!" And thank God for the victory we ultimately won at San Jacinto over Santa Anna and his army.

Texans love their beef, as well, and March 2 is as fine a time as any to barbecue a brisket, and serve it up with cob corn, potato salad, coleslaw, and a few onion slices and jalapeños.

If you want to go all out for your Texas Independence Day celebration, pull out your cowboy hats and boots or dress in buckskins. Decorate with red, white, and blue tablecloths, lots of bluebonnets and a few lone stars.

You might even hang a cannon flag with a "Come and Take It" taunt scrawled across it. Read William Barrett Travis's "Victory or Death" letter aloud (or, better yet, commit it to memory and quote it in unison).

-42-
Feed Me, I'm Irish!

For over twenty-five years now, our family has celebrated St. Patrick's Day with a "Leprechaun Lunch."

The menu varies slightly year to year (depending on the age and pickiness of my little eaters and my own current stage of pregnancy or post partum-ness), but the theme remains the same: everything's green!

Here is a sampling of dishes we've served in the past:

- white grapes (they *look* green)
- sugar snap peas (raw)
- parmesan asparagus (recipe on p. 143)
- chicken wraps (made with spinach & green tortillas)
- split pea soup
- broccoli salad (recipe on p. 111)
- spinach quiche
- guacamole (served with tortilla chips—see p. 114)
- zucchini rounds and celery sticks (w/ranch dressing)
- clover-leaf cookies with green sugar sprinkles

And to wash it all down, I make a pitcher of Paddy's Punch. To make it, just mix ½ gallon lime sherbet with a 2-liter bottle of ginger ale. Cheers!

Section 7: Holiday Happenings

-43-
Don't Be Fooled

When you have as many kids as we do, you can count on being tricked multiple times on April Fool's Day. My children are pretty clever, and I've always been a sucker for their shenanigans.

Fortunately, mealtime gives Mom a wonderful opportunity to turn the tables, so to speak. Pinterest abounds with fun ideas for dressing up main courses to look like dessert and styling dessert to look like a main course.

Try one of these simple ideas below or search the Internet for more elaborate ideas for fooling your family over dinner:

- Bake miniature meatloaves in a muffin tin and top with mashed potato "icing" to make faux cupcakes

- Make "grilled cheese sandwiches" using two slices of pound cake stuck together with yellow icing

- Make a "hot caramel sundae" using mashed potatoes and brown gravy in a parfait glass, topped with a piece of red bell pepper cut in the shape of a cherry

- Fashion our no-bake chocolate oatmeal cookie dough into the shape of chopped steak and serve with a scoop of ice cream and caramel made to resemble a side of mashed potatoes and gravy

-44-
Christ is Risen Indeed!

For a hands-on reminder of Jesus' self-sacrificing love, bake a batch of "resurrection cookies" with your kids:

1 cup pecan halves	a pinch of salt
1 tsp vinegar	1 cup of sugar
3 eggs	

Preheat oven to 300°. Put pecans into zipper bag and beat with a wooden spoon until broken into small pieces. Recall how Jesus was beaten before His death. (Matt. 27:27-30)

Let your child smell the vinegar as you explain how Jesus was given vinegar to drink on the cross. (Matt. 27:48) Separate eggs; add whites to the vinegar. Discuss how eggs represent the new life Jesus came to give us. (2 Cor. 5:17)

Sprinkle salt on your child's hand and recall the salty tears Christ's followers shed after his death (Luke 23:27). Brush the salt into the bowl; add sugar to represent the sweetest part of the story—Jesus gave His life because He loves us! (Romans 5:8) Beat egg white mixture on high 12-15 minutes until stiff and white, telling how Jesus' blood washes us white as snow.(Isa.1:18) Fold in nuts. Drop by rounded teaspoons on wax paper covered cookie sheets to represent the tomb where Jesus lay. Place in oven, turn it OFF, seal the door shut with masking tape. (Matt. 27:57-66) Go to bed, then check cookies Easter morning. When you crack them open, they'll be empty—just like the tomb!

Section 7: Holiday Happenings

-45-
Cinco de Mayo Fiesta

So what if *Cinco de Mayo* is a bigger deal in the US than it is in Mexico? We love underdog stories, we're proud of our southern neighbor's David-and-Goliath win over the French at the Battle of Puebla (in 1862), and we enjoy a good Fiesta as much as the next guy.

We're also happy for any excuse to eat Mexican cuisine.

Our daughters, Rebekah and Rachel, really get into the spirit of this holiday and spend hours pressing homemade tortillas, chopping onions, tomatoes, peppers, and avocados, and preparing authentic dishes for our family to feast upon.

The results are mouthwatering.

If you'd be interested in whipping up some terrific Tex-Mex to mark the day (maybe not as "authentic" as what our girls cook, but definitely delicious), you'll find recipes for the following family favorites on the pages listed:

- Savor-it-Slowly Guacamole—p. 114
- Chicken Tortilla Soup—p. 107
- Taco Soup—p. 105
- Easy Cheesy Enchiladas—p. 122
- King Ranch Chicken—p. 121

Es muy rico… so eat up and enjoy the fiesta!

Sit Down & Eat

-46-
Fourth of July Picnic

When most people plan Independence Day celebrations, they think *fireworks*. That's why the party doesn't start until late afternoon, so the explosive display can be seen against the night sky.

We like to start our Fourth of July celebrations in the morning with a neighborhood parade—kids decorate their bikes and wagons with flags and posters and red, white, and blue streamers, and we all line up behind the neighborhood vets who carry the flag to lead our processional.

When we first moved to East Texas, we started leaving invitations to an Independence Day Block Party in all the mailboxes up and down our street. We anticipated having lots of young families show up for the festivities, but it was mainly senior citizens who congregated in our yard year after year. We loved getting to know them!

As for food, that was easy. We told everybody to bring a 2-liter soda, a package of franks, and a couple of lawn chairs. We provided buns and condiments, paper goods, potato salad, and watermelon for dessert. Of course, we could have supplied the drinks and hot dogs, too, but we've discovered over the years that more people show up when they're allowed to contribute to the meal.

Section 7: Holiday Happenings

-47-
Cow Appreciation Day

It only happens once a year, usually in the second week of July. Sometimes on Tuesday. Sometimes on Friday. We mark our calendars early and never miss it.

It's Cow Appreciation Day at Chick-fil-A! Any customer who shows up sporting a cow costume will be rewarded with a free entrée—isn't that "udderly" amazing?

If you don't already have a closet full of cowhide handy, don't worry. Chick-fil-A's got you covered. They make it easy for folks to participate with a handy "cow starter kit." (To download your free printable costume, follow this link: http://www.chick-fil-a.com/media/pdf/cow_starter_kit.pdf)

We printed out a big stack of the signs, ears, noses, and tails in the starter kit back when we first "herd" about this promotion, laminated them, and have been using them ever since—only now we wear matching hand-painted T-shirts and baseball caps, as well. Our kids enjoy adding new touches to our costumes every year.

So grab your horns and hooves and moooove on over to your nearest Chick-fil-A next July. Maybe our family will "spot" you there!

-48-
Thanksgiving Bounty

According to the diary of Governor William Bradford, during the famine of 1623, the settlers of Plymouth were forced to subsist for several days at a time on just a few grains of corn.

In remembrance of those lean times, guests at our family's Thanksgiving Day celebrations often find five kernels of corn beside their plate. And at some point during the meal, we take turns naming five things for which we're thankful that year—one for each kernel. It's a fun way to help keep the day's focus where it should be. Whether you gather hand-in-hand with loved ones to pray for God's blessing on your Thanksgiving meal or you go around the table individually afterwards and express gratitude for blessings already bestowed, we hope your holiday will not only be a day of feeling generally thankful, but of giving specific thanks to God, from whom all blessings flow:

"Every good thing bestowed and every perfect gift is from above, coming down from the Father of lights, with whom there is no variation or shifting shadow." James 1:17 NASB

"Enter into His gates with thanksgiving, and into His courts with praise: be thankful unto Him, and bless His name." Psalm 100:4

Section 7: Holiday Happenings

-49-
Christmas Morning

Growing up, my family usually traveled to Oklahoma to spend Christmas day at my grandparents' house, so we celebrated "Christmas" at home a day early. And since we had to hit the road pretty soon after the gifts were opened, we'd momentarily forgo turkey and dressing in favor of a bountiful breakfast.

Even today, Christmas doesn't seem like Christmas without those traditional dishes I grew up enjoying with my family. Side dishes varied—some years Mom made sausage balls and blueberry muffins, other years she'd serve smoky links and buttermilk biscuits—but the main course never varied.

What was this pièce de résistance, you may ask? It was a piping hot egg casserole. (You'll find the recipe on p. 86.) The ham makes it hearty; half-and-half makes it fluffy.

Other regulars on our Christmas morning menu were milk, orange juice, and some sort of fruit salad, which often featured one of the following combinations:

- sliced bananas, strawberries, and canned peaches
- a medley of watermelon, cantaloupe, and honeydew
- pineapple, oranges, grapes, and shredded coconut
- strawberries, blueberries, and blackberries

Section 8

★ Making the Ordinary Extra-Ordinary ★

Section 8: Making the Ordinary Extra-Ordinary

-50-
Theme Dinners

When our children were little, we spent one week of the summer at "Family Camp" for several years running.

The thing I loved most about Family Camp was the fact that somebody else did all the cooking.

The thing my kids loved most was that camp dinners usually featured some wacky theme: Cowboys and Indians. Favorite Sports Teams. 50's Sock Hop. Every night, it was something new and different.

One summer, the camp hosted an especially memorable "flip-flop night." Parents were instructed to come to dinner dressed as their children and children were told to come dressed as their parents. Our little guys wore pint-sized hospital scrubs. Their dad wore a giant homemade onesie. He looked so funny!

Fortunately, you don't have to go away for camp to make great mealtime memories with your family. This section is chock full of ideas for themed meals. Some of them focus on the food being served, some on the people doing the dining, and some on both. So try one soon and bring a little camp time fun to your own dinner table.

Sit Down & Eat

-51-
We Call It Bella Notte

Want to make an Italian dinner extra special? Try adding a little ambiance, à la *Lady and the Tramp.*

A red checkered tablecloth, some drippy candles, and a little Frank Sinatra music crooning in the background is all you need.

Incidentally, if you—like me—have ever wondered why so many Italian places seem to play the same Sinatra soundtrack, I think it's because Frank's parents were Italian immigrants. (No upcharge for that tidbit of trivia.☺)

This authentic, romantic atmosphere will improve the taste of almost any dish you prepare, but to continue the theme, try making spaghetti with meat sauce (p. 124), layered lasagna (p. 135), or maybe even manicotti (I normally just use the recipe on the pasta package for that one). Or go easy on the cook and bring home a few pizzas!

To accompany the meal, serve crusty garlic toast or soft, warm breadsticks, with herbed olive oil for dipping. You'll also want a big tossed salad: iceberg lettuce, tomato wedges, salad peppers, olives, croutons, and tangy Italian dressing. For dessert, consider serving creamy cheesecake with cherry or chocolate sauce. *Buon Appetito!*

Section 8: Making the Ordinary Extra-Ordinary

-52-
South of the Border

Living as our family does in Texas, Mexican food is a staple part of our diet. Taco Tuesdays. Fajita Fridays. A Tex-Mex restaurant on every corner. The food is fantastic, but I also love all the bright festive colors that adorn most of these establishments.

For a fun theme dinner, bring some of that brightness home.
A woven Mexican blanket with colorful stripes can serve double-duty as a table cloth. For a centerpiece, use a *piñata* or a bright bouquet of homemade tissue paper flowers. To make these bright blossoms, simply fold three or four layers of red, yellow, blue, or purple tissue paper back and forth, accordion style, secure in the middle with a green pipe cleaner stem, then gently separate layers to create each bloom.

Alternatively, you can cut small diamonds and triangles into your accordion folds to make *papel picado* flags, then string them together overhead for an authentic looking Mexican banner.

Check out the suggestions in Chapter 45 (p. 65) for menu ideas, then serve them up wearing sombreros, ponchos, or embroidered dresses while lively *fiesta de musica* plays in the background. *Olé!*

Sit Down & Eat

-53-
Chop Suey

My husband took me out for a hibachi dinner date recently, and the other people at our table complimented our deft use of chopsticks. "Where did you learn to do that?" they wanted to know.

The answer? We first visited a hibachi grill on our honeymoon, and my husband thought it would be fun to eat the entire meal with chopsticks, so we did (albeit very awkwardly). With every bite, more food fell back to our plate than made it to our mouth. But after 30 years of practicing every time we go out for Asian food of any sort, we've steadily improved so that now we're both very comfortable and adept at eating with chopsticks.

Doug eventually bought chopsticks for everybody in the family, so the kids could get regular practice, too. And what better time to use them, than for a theme meal featuring Asian cooking? Stir fry some veggies, brown some pepper steak, steam some rice, and maybe even serve up a little sushi. There's also egg rolls, spring rolls, cashew chicken, wonton soup—truly something for every taste, and fairly easy to prepare.

Complete the theme by dressing in bathrobe "kimonos," decorating with paper lanterns (store bought or handmade), and playing Asian music during dinner.

Section 8: Making the Ordinary Extra-Ordinary

-54-
Hawaiian Luau

Aloha! Let's break out the leis, grass skirts, muumuus, tropical prints and tiki torches, and get ready for an old-fashioned Hawaiian luau. Combining a little culture study with traditional dishes and music will make this theme dinner even more memorable.

For dinner, try grilling mahi-mahi or chicken kabobs or maybe even a little Spam.

Did you know that Spam (short for "spiced ham," that potted meat in the blue rectangular tin) is considered a delicacy in Hawaii? They consume more Spam there than in any other state of the union—7 million cans a year—having gotten hooked on it during World War II when GIs received regular rations of the salty luncheon meat, since it had a long shelf life and required no refrigeration.

To compliment the main course, mix up a batch of tropical fruit salad, warm some Hawaiian bread rolls, fry a little rice, and mix up an ice cold pitcher of tea with pineapple and lemongrass.

As for after dinner entertainment, crank up a recording of "The Hukilau Song" and try your hands (and hips) at hula dancing.

-55-
Color Coded Meals

I've already written about the green-themed meals we eat on St. Patrick's day, but it's possible to do the same thing with other colors, as well. The best part is that some of the brightest foods you can eat are raw fruits and vegetables, which make for pretty healthful meals.

Here are a few ideas for monochromatic dining. How many more foods can you think of under each heading?

RED: strawberries, red bell peppers, watermelon, radishes, cherry tomatoes, tomato soup, chili beans, etc.

ORANGE: tangerines, carrots, sweet potatoes, cantaloupe, cheddar cheese, orange bell peppers, peaches, apricots, etc.

YELLOW: bananas, pineapple, golden potatoes, macaroni & cheese, yellow bell peppers, squash, etc.

GREEN: kiwi, celery, zucchini, broccoli, Brussels sprouts, white grapes, split pea soup, pesto, kale, spinach, salad, etc.

PURPLE: red grapes, beets, egg plant, plums, purple sweet potatoes, red cabbage, red onions, etc.

WHITE: cauliflower, turnips, mushrooms, mashed potatoes, white radishes, cream cheese, potato rolls, etc.

Section 8: Making the Ordinary Extra-Ordinary

-56-
Costume Dinners

Even the simplest of meals is more memorable when the people eating it do so in costume. When you ask kids to come to to the table dressed as some famous figure, you never know who'll show up for dinner.

For best results, parents and house guests should dress up, too. To make things really interesting, have each person tell something interesting about the person they're portraying. Here are a few ideas to get you started...come to dinner dressed as your favorite:

- superhero
- book character
- biblical figure
- political personality
- movie star or musician
- Disney prince or princess

Alternatively, instead of adopting the dress of a specific person, try dressing in the garb of your favorite:

- sports team
- nation or country
- historical era
- zoo animal

Section 9

Breakfast of Champions

Section 9: Breakfast of Champions

-57-
Teddy Bear Toast

I don't know what happens at your house, but sometimes at ours, I take a break and let the kids make breakfast.

This dish—which our children have affectionately dubbed "Teddy Bear Toast"—is pretty self-explanatory. It's fun. It's tasty. It's easy to make. And it's actually very nutritious. You don't even have to have little ones at home to enjoy it.

Ingredients:
whole wheat bread
creamy peanut butter
1 banana, sliced
raisins/ chocolate chips

Directions:
Toast bread until it's golden. Spread peanut butter on top while toast is still warm. Place two slices of banana in the upper corners (for ears) and one in the middle (for muzzle). Add two raisins or chocolate chips for eyes, just above the center slice, and another for the nose on top of the banana snout.

And that's it! Now eat and enjoy (or if you are making this as a surprise treat for your mama, serve her a slice for breakfast in bed)!

Sit Down & Eat

-58-
Egg Muffins

A friend of mine made our family a batch of these the week we brought our seventh baby home from the hospital. We enjoyed them so much, we requested the recipe and were shocked to learn how easy they are to make. We've been cooking them regularly ever since.

> 1 can of flaky-style biscuits
> 3-5 eggs
> 5-6 slices of luncheon meat (we use smoked turkey)
> 1/2 cup grated cheese
> salt & pepper (to taste)

Preheat the oven to 350°F. Spray two full-size muffins tins with nonstick cooking spray.

One wonderful thing about this recipe is that it stretches so far: You'll only need one can of eight flaky-layer style biscuits to make twenty-four muffins. Carefully divide each biscuit into three pieces by separating the layers, then use each piece to line a cup of your muffin tin. Roll up your luncheon meat and slice into thin strips. Divide the shredded meat evenly between the muffins tins and add a pinch of shredded cheese on top of the meat. Beat eggs with salt and pepper, then spoon just enough into each cup to moisten other ingredients. Bake for 12-15 minutes or until tops are golden. Serve with cold milk and fresh fruit. Enjoy!

Section 9: Breakfast of Champions

-59-
Fresh Fruit Smoothies

Fresh fruit smoothies are easy to make, delicious to drink, and really good for you. It's like drinking a milkshake for breakfast, only without the guilt. ☺

My daughter is particularly fond of smoothies and drinks at least one a day. It's a smart way to work in a few extra servings of fruit and veggies.

Try some of these great combinations (freeze the fruit in advance, then add milk or juice to make blending easier):

- watermelon, strawberries, and orange juice
- strawberries, bananas, and almond milk
- mango, pineapple, and coconut milk
- strawberries, spinach, banana, and almond milk
- bananas, peanut butter, and vanilla yogurt
- bananas, cocoa powder, peanut butter, and yogurt
- blueberries, strawberries, raspberries, and water

For a breakfast that will stick to your ribs a little longer, add oats or flax powder to any of the above combinations. Greens are also a healthful addition; you can add a handful of spinach and hardly even notice. Kale is also a good choice, though it has a stronger flavor and is harder to "sneak" in without the veggie-phobes realizing it's there.

Sit Down & Eat

-60-
Breakfast Casserole

I first tasted this casserole at a brunch my Sunday School teacher hosted for our junior high girls' class. It was the dish their family traditionally ate on Christmas morning, and pretty soon, our family was doing the same. By mixing it up a day ahead of time and letting it sit in the refrigerator overnight, you save time and mess the next morning. Plus, it's delicious—light and fluffy and full of flavor.

- 2 ½ cups turkey ham
- 2 cups grated cheddar cheese
- 1 dozen eggs
- ¼ cup butter
- 1 cup half & half
- ½ tsp salt
- dash pepper
- 2 tsp dried mustard

Spray 9" x13" baking dish with non-stick spray. Layer in pan: meat, then cheese, then the rest of the ingredients, combined (with eggs slightly beaten). Bake at 325° for 35 to 45 minutes or until light golden brown. Pair it with biscuits, jelly, and a fresh fruit salad for a well-balanced and filling breakfast. This dish is a great choice for serving to overnight houseguests—in December or any month of the year!

Section 9: Breakfast of Champions

-61-
Homemade Granola

Granola made from scratch is much healthier and tastier than the store bought variety—at least, in my opinion. We go through it so fast, I'd make a double or triple batch of this recipe if I could find a big enough pan to cook it in!

6 cups of rolled oats
2 cups shredded coconut
2 cups nuts (pecans, almonds, sunflower seeds, etc.)
1 tsp salt
1 cup coconut oil or butter
3 Tbsp vanilla
1 cup honey
1½ cups dried fruit (raisins, craisins, apricots, etc.)

Combine oats, coconut, nuts, and salt in a deep pan. In a separate bowl, whisk together oil, vanilla, and honey, then drizzle over dry ingredients, stirring to coat lightly. Place in a 250° oven for 1 ½ hours, turning mixture thoroughly every 15 minutes until oats are light golden brown.

Remove from oven and turn thoroughly again. Let cool completely before adding raisins, dates, or other dried fruit. Store in an airtight container in a cool, dry place. It should keep for a couple of weeks, but ours never lasts that long.

-62-
Ice Cream for Breakfast

My father used to feed me and my sister ice cream for breakfast (unbeknownst to my mom, who would have been mortified to think Dad was sending us to school with cookies-n-cream dribbled down the fronts of our dresses). He always claimed an ice cream cone was no different than a bowl of sugar-coated cereal with milk.

Even as an adult, I have a hard time arguing with that ironclad logic. And so, *occasionally*, I feed my kids ice cream for breakfast, too—but not without a twinge of guilt consuming them. If Mom found out, would she disapprove?

I can now lay all those concerns aside. Recent scientific studies indicate eating ice cream early in the morning is actually beneficial to the brain. People who eat ice cream for breakfast have been shown to process information more efficiently than those who don't. They're also more alert and energetic and have better reaction times. An official holiday has even been set aside to encourage the practice: National "Eat Ice Cream for Breakfast Day."

All that to say, my dad was obviously ahead of his time. Far from being overly-permissive, he was simply doing his part to ensure my sister and I performed well in school. Perhaps I should follow his lead and feed my kids ice cream for breakfast more often.... How early does Braum's open?

Section 9: Breakfast of Champions

-63-
Blueberry Muffins

Our family goes berry picking every summer. We pick all we can and freeze what we don't eat immediately. This is one of our favorite things to do with the extras:

> 2½ cups of flour
> 2 cups of rolled oats
> 1 cup brown sugar
> 4 tsp of baking powder
> 1 tsp of salt
> 2 eggs
> ½ cup coconut oil
> 1½ cups almond milk
> 2 cups blueberries (fresh or frozen)

Variations: Instead of blueberries, substitute
> 2 cups of nuts (or)
> 2 cups of chocolate chips (or)
> 1 cup diced apples, ½ cup raisins, and ½ cup walnuts

Preheat oven to 400°F. Grease muffin tins or use paper liners. Mix dry ingredients thoroughly. Combine milk, oil, vanilla, and well-beaten eggs. Stir into dry ingredients just until batter is moistened (batter will be lumpy). Fold in blueberries (or chocolate chips, nuts, etc.). Spoon into prepared muffin tins, about 3/4 full. Bake 20-22 minutes or until tops just begin to brown. Makes 2 dozen muffins.

Sit Down & Eat

-64-
Cooked-to-Order Pancakes

With this one basic batter, you can prepare enough custom-made pancakes to satisfy the entire family. We double the recipe to feed our family of ten. If I were making them when our older kids were in town, I'd triple it.

2 cups flour
2 tsp baking powder
½ tsp salt
1½ Tbsp sugar
2 eggs
2 cups milk
butter for cooking
optional: nuts, berries, etc.

These are delicious plain, or you can spruce them up by mixing in any of the following ingredients before cooking: nuts, blueberries, chocolate chips, cranberries, &/or coconut.

In a large mixing bowl, combine all dry ingredients. Beat milk and eggs together, then add to the dry ingredients and mix gently until everything is just moistened. Don't worry if the batter is lumpy—pancakes will turn out better if you don't overwork it.

Melt a little butter on a medium hot griddle, then ladle batter on as soon as butter stops foaming. When the center of the pancake begins to bubble, flip it over and brown the other side. Serve with hot maple syrup.

Section 9: Breakfast of Champions

-65-
Sticky Buns

Mmm-mmm! Whenever we make sticky buns, our house gets filled with the most scrumptious smell. They're super easy, and my family loves them.

What's more, they're fun to make, and little helpers can easily get in on the "shake-and-bake" action:

> 2 tubes of flaky biscuits
> 1/2 cup butter (melted)
> 4 Tbsp pancake syrup
> 1/2 cup packed brown sugar
> 3/4 cup chopped pecans (optional)
> 1/4 cup sugar
> 1 1/2 tsp cinnamon

Preheat oven to 375°F. Spray 2 muffin tins with non-stick cooking spray. Combine the melted butter, syrup, brown sugar and nuts in a small bowl, then spoon into bottom of muffin tins. Set aside.

Combine white sugar and cinnamon in a ziplock bag. Cut biscuits into small pieces (6-8 pieces per biscuit). Drop all the pieces into the bag of cinnamon sugar, seal, and shake, then open bag and transfer coated pieces into muffin tins. Bake at 375° for 15-18 minutes. Serve warm with a tall glass of cold milk. Yum!

Section 10

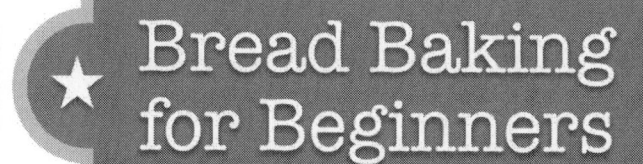

Bread Baking for Beginners

Section 10: Bread Baking for Beginners

-66-
Homemade vs. Store Bought

I love the smell of fresh homemade bread as much as the next person, and—for cents on the dollar—can bake a loaf at home that's tastier and more healthful than the majority of bagged and sliced varieties carried by the corner grocer.

Nevertheless, life is busy. Time does not allow the luxury of baking bread at home. We have enough to worry about without feeling guilty for serving store-bought bread!

If baking is your thing, go for it. That will undoubtedly add a lot of luscious kitchen smells to your children's stash of fond memories. Teach them how to bake while you're at it, so they'll have an easier time continuing the tradition with their own families in the future.

If, however, you feel lost in a kitchen and have no desire to grind your own grain or knead your own dough—if your culinary skills are more likely to make eyes water from acrid smoke than mouths water with delectable aromas—then savor the fact that reasonable alternatives exist. Rest in the knowledge that your kids can have strong, healthy bodies and wonderful childhood memories, even if you never master (or even attempt) the mysterious art of bread baking.

Sit Down & Eat

-67-
Garlic Bread

It's hard to beat a crusty loaf of Italian bread as a side to nearly any main dish. When I think of pulling it warm from the oven, its sides slathered in garlic butter, I can almost smell it, and my mouth immediately starts to water.

To save time, we butter our bread in advance. I melt a stick of butter, stir in about a quarter teaspoon of garlic powder and a pinch or two of dried parsley, then spoon and spread it on one side of each slice of bread.

For soft bread, I leave the buttered slices in the shape of the original loaf and wrap it in aluminum foil before popping it into a 350° oven for 5-10 minutes.

For crispier bread, increase the oven temperature to 400° and toast the slices butter-side up for 3-5 minutes.

Those who prefer to eat a plant-based diet can use olive oil instead of butter.

Section 10: Bread Baking for Beginners

-68-
Cheddar Biscuits

Red Lobster has long been one of my husband's favorite restaurants. Half of our kids are thrilled anytime he suggests we eat there, while the other half lobby for Mexican food, instead. But on one thing we all agree: their cheddar biscuits are the best. This recipe comes closer to approximating the taste than any other we've tried:

2 cups flour	¼ cup shortening
2 Tbsp baking powder	4 Tbsp butter, sliced
2½ tsp sugar	1¼ cups grated cheddar
¼ tsp salt	¾ cup milk

Preheat oven to 425°F. Combine dry ingredients in food processor. Add shortening; pulse until combined. Add butter; pulse until it's broken into pea-size pieces. Add cheese. Pulse a few times more. Pour in milk. Pulse just enough to moisten mixture. Turn onto clean surface and knead into a ball without overworking.

Drop onto baking sheet in scant ¼-cup portions, 2 inches apart, then bake until golden on the center rack in pre-heated oven. Remove from oven, brush with garlic butter (recipe follows) and serve warm. They won't last long!

¼ cup of butter
1 clove garlic, minced
1 tsp dried parsley

Cook butter and garlic over medium heat until butter is just melted, then add parsley

-69-
Whole Wheat Bread

If you do lots of baking, you may want to invest in a grain mill for optimal taste and nutrition. Otherwise, go for whole grain flours in the grocer's aisle. Any of them will be an improvement over the highly processed, bleached variety. There's more truth in that old adage, "The whiter the bread, the sooner you're dead," than most of us realize. If your family is accustomed to soft, white, doughy bread, you may have to wean them onto whole wheat gradually. This easy-to-make recipe can help you do just that:

3 cups warm water
2 pkg active dry yeast
1/3 + 1/3 cups honey
5 cups bread flour

3 Tbsp + 2 Tbsp butter
1 Tbsp salt
3½ cups whole wheat flour

In large mixing bowl, combine warm (110°) water, yeast, 1/3 cup honey, and 5 cups bread flour. Stir and let sit until big and bubbly. Mix in another 1/3 cup honey, 3 tablespoons of melted butter, salt, and 2 cups of whole wheat flour. Mix on medium speed (or knead on floured counter), adding more whole wheat flour ½ cup at a time until dough begins to pull away from edge of bowl (or countertop). Cover with dishtowel and let rise in a warm place until doubled in size. Punch down. Divide into 3 loaves. Shape in pans. Let rise again until it tops the pans. Bake at 350° for 25-30 minutes. Brush tops of baked loaves with melted butter, then cool.

Section 10: Bread Baking for Beginners

-70-
Banana Nut Bread

Our family used to make banana nut bread or banana nut muffins almost weekly. Sometimes I'd buy several pounds of overripe bananas specifically for that purpose and make enough loaves to freeze or share with neighbors.

I kept the recipe taped inside a kitchen cabinet door for easy reference. Unfortunately, when we moved a few years ago, that recipe got left behind. My daughter soon found a replacement recipe on the back of a package of Land O' Lakes butter, and we like it even better than the original. The loaves come out crisp and brown on the outside, soft and sweet on the inside, like banana nut bread should be.

- 1 1/4 cup sugar
- 1 cup butter, softened
- 4 ripe bananas, mashed
- 2 cup walnuts, chopped
- 1/2 tsp ground cinnamon
- 3 cups flour
- 1 tsp vanilla
- 4 eggs
- 1 tsp baking soda
- 1 tsp salt

Preheat oven to 350°F. Grease and flour two 8×4-inch loaf pans; set aside. Using mixer, combine sugar, butter and eggs in bowl at medium speed, scraping bowl often, until creamy. Add mashed banana and vanilla to bread batter, then stir in all remaining ingredients, then fold in nuts. Spoon batter into prepared loaf pans. Bake about 1 hour, cool 10 minutes, then enjoy while bread is still warm. Makes 2 loaves.

Section 11

Soup's On

Section 11: Soup's On

-71-
Marvelous Minestrone

This is just the dish for when the temperatures begin to dip. Full of healthful vegetables and clear broth, it has a wonderful flavor that our family loves.

- 1 pkg beef smoked sausage
- 1 onion
- 2 tsp minced garlic
- 3-4 zucchini
- 3-4 carrots
- 1 head of green cabbage, shredded
- 8-10 cups beef stock (or water with bouillon)
- 1 can diced tomatoes
- 1 can great northern beans
- 2 tsp Italian seasoning
- salt and pepper to taste

Sauté onion with thinly-sliced sausage until transparent. Add minced garlic, sliced zucchini and carrots, and shredded cabbage. Sauté a few minutes longer, then add beef stock, seasonings, and tomatoes, and bring to a boil. Reduce heat and simmer for at least an hour. Add beans just before serving.

Hint: This recipe doubles easily and can also be frozen. Warm it in a crock-pot the second time around and serve with fresh bread or crackers for a truly fuss-free meal.

Sit Down & Eat

-72-
Chicken and Noodles

Every time I make this soup, I think of my father. It's a recipe he made often when I was growing up, especially if anybody in the family was sick. Whenever I was the one under the weather, this got me to feeling better quickly.

> 2-3 large chicken breasts
> 1 yellow onion
> 3-4 carrots, sliced
> 3-4 stalks celery, sliced
> 6-8 cups chicken stock
> garlic, salt and pepper to taste
> 1 can cream of chicken soup
> 1 10-12 oz package egg noodles

Sauté diced onion and cubed chicken breast over med-high heat until chicken is done. (I usually keep about 3-5 lbs of chicken breasts marinating in a bottle of Italian salad dressing in the refrigerator at all times. This is what I use for making soup and casseroles or grilling).

Add carrots, celery and chicken stock (use homemade stock, canned, or bouillon cubes—whatever you have on hand). Bring to a boil. Add seasonings, stir in noodles, and reduce heat to lowest setting. Cover and let sit 10-15 minutes. Stir in cream of chicken soup to thicken base (optional) and serve with saltine crackers or wheat thins.

Section 11: Soup's On

-73-
Taco Soup

This quick and easy recipe takes only a few minutes to throw together. I always keep the ingredients on hand in case unexpected company drops by.

- 1 can of Ranch Style Beans
- 1 can of black beans
- 1 can of great northern beans
- 1 can of garbanzo beans
- 1 can of kidney beans
- 1 can of Rotel diced tomatoes with green chilies
- 1-2 lbs of ground beef, browned
- 1 diced onion
- 1 pkg. taco seasoning mix
- crackers or chips
- sour cream (optional)
- grated cheese

In a large stew pot, sauté the onions and brown the ground beef, if it's not already cooked, then dump in all the cans of beans, plus a little extra water. Heat for at least 15-20 minutes.

Eat the soup with crackers or pour it over tortilla chips and top with grated cheese, sour cream, and diced onions. For a healthier vegan version, omit the meat and dairy.

-74-
Garlicky Lentils

Lentils require no soaking and are extremely quick to prepare (they cook in six minutes flat when I use a pressure cooker, but even on the stovetop, they're done in half an hour). I love that about them.

I also love the fact that lentils are so good for you. And they're delicious, to boot, especially in this family favorite:

> 1 yellow onion
> 2 cups lentils
> 1 cup of carrots
> 6-8 cloves of garlic
> 12-14 cups water
> 4 Tbsp olive oil
> 4 Tbsp red wine vinegar
> 1 tsp oregeno
> 8 cubes of beef bouillon
> 4 bay leaves
> salt & pepper to taste

Dice the onion, mince the garlic, and slice the carrots into rounds. Combine with all remaining ingredients in a soup pot. Bring to a boil, then simmer 30-40 minutes. For a vegan version, use vegetable stock instead of beef bouillon and water. Remove the bay leaves before serving.

Section 11: Soup's On

-75-
Chicken Tortilla Soup

I usually make this soup the day after we eat King Ranch Chicken (p. 121) and add whatever is left of the casserole to the pot, but it is delicious even without that extra flavor.

- 2-3 chicken breasts
- 1 yellow onion, diced
- dash of olive oil
- 2-3 yellow squash, sliced
- 2-3 zucchini squash, sliced
- 1 can hominy
- 1 can rotel tomatoes
- 12 cups chicken broth (or water with boullion)
- 1-2 Tbsp dried cilantro
- salt and pepper
- 2-3 ripe avocados, sliced
- grated cheddar cheese
- sour cream (optional)
- tortilla chips

Sauté onion and chicken until chicken is cooked and onion is translucent. Add canned vegetables and sliced squash, seasonings, and broth or water. Bring to a boil. Turn heat down and simmer until squash is tender. Serve over chips, and garnish with avocado slices, cheese, and sour cream.

Section 12

Rabbit Food

Section 12: Rabbit Food

-76-
Broccoli Cauliflower Salad

A dear friend of mine invited me to lunch almost three decades ago and prepared this salad to go with our meal. I ate three servings and asked for the recipe, which she graciously shared. My family has been eating it with enthusiasm ever since (with the exception of my husband, who loves bacon, but is not overly fond of cauliflower, so I usually serve it when he's not at home).

>1 head of iceberg lettuce, torn into small pieces
>2 cups of broccoli florets, chopped small
>2 cups of cauliflower florets, chopped small
>1/2 red onion, sliced paper thin
>3-4 strips of thick sliced bacon, fried crispy and crumbled
>1 cup mayonnaise
>1 cup sugar
>1 cup parmesan cheese

Mix last three ingredients to make dressing, set aside.

Wash and dry lettuce and vegetables, then chop, slice, and tear into pieces per directions. Combine in a large mixing bowl. Add bacon, then toss with dressing until thoroughly coated. Transfer to salad bowl and serve immediately.

-77-
Tex-Mex Salad

My mom made this salad regularly when I was growing up. Her recipe called for the lettuce to be tossed with Catalina dressing. If you like your salad sweet, then you may want to try that, but in my opinion, it ruins the taste—which is why Mother usually made a separate bowl for me, without the dressing.

Layer the following ingredients in a clear salad bowl:

> 1 head of lettuce, rinsed, dried, and torn in pieces
> 2 tomatoes, diced
> 6-8 slices of bacon, fried and crumbled
> 1 can of ranch style beans
> 2-3 cups of Fritos corn chips, crumbled
> 1 cup of grated cheddar cheese
> sprinkle the top with chopped green onion

Do not toss until you are ready to serve. The salad looks very pretty layered in the bowl.

It really has plenty of flavor with no dressing at all, but if you must add a topping, try a spoonful of picante sauce or maybe even a dollop of sour cream, instead.

Section 12: Rabbit Food

-78-
All-American Potato Salad

Looking for a good side dish for your Memorial Day picnic? You'd have a hard time doing better than a pot of baked beans, some ice-cold watermelon, and a big batch of our All-American Potato Salad. Whether you serve it hot or cold, it's sure to be a crowd pleaser!

- 10 red potatoes
- 5 eggs
- 1 red onion, diced
- 1½ cups mayonnaise
- 4 Tbsp dill pickle relish
- 3 Tbsp mustard
- 1½ tsp salt
- ¼ tsp ground black pepper
- ¼ tsp paprika

Scrub and dice potatoes (I usually leave the skins on), then boil until fork tender. Drain and place in a large mixing bowl. In a separate pan, boil eggs until hard, then cool, peel, dice, and transfer to the same bowl. Chop onion and add to potato mixture, then stir in mayonnaise, dill pickle relish, mustard, salt and pepper. Blend until potatoes are thoroughly coated, but still chunky. Our family likes to eat it while it's still hot, but it tastes great chilled, as well.

-79-
Savor-It-Slowly Guacamole

As you've probably gathered by now, our family loves Tex-Mex food—even the babies. One of our little ones spurned all the puréed baby food we proffered, but would eat her weight in refried beans and guacamole!

This recipe is simple enough that a six-year-old can make it, but the results are scrumptious. The packaged stuff you get at the store really can't compare in taste and quality to homemade. Try it yourself and see:

- 4 large ripe avocados
- 1 small lime, juiced
- 1 small onion, minced
- 1 medium tomato, diced
- 1 tsp salt
- 1 tsp minced garlic
- 2 tsp cilantro
- 1 pinch of red pepper flakes (to taste)

Halve, seed, and cube avocados. Place in mixing bowl. Drizzle lime juice over all, then add onions, salt, and spices. Stir together with spoon until consistently mixed. Fold in the tomatoes, then serve with crisp tortilla chips or on warm corn tortillas.

Guacamole is never as good the second day, so dig in and down it all!

Section 12: Rabbit Food

-80-
Mom's Signature Salad

This is my family's favorite salad. I especially like to make it whenever my husband grills. It goes well with chicken, fish, or steak. Just add a loaded baked potato on the side, plus a couple of crusty loaves of French bread, and you're good to go!

    1 lb. mixed baby greens
    1 ripe avocado, diced
    1 cup grape tomatoes, cut into halves
    ½ red onion, sliced paper thin
    ½ cup coarsely chopped pecans or pistachios
    ½ cup crumbled blue cheese
    freshly ground black pepper, to taste
    olive oil and red wine vinegar, to taste

Combine ingredients in a large salad bowl (I usually double or triple this recipe and serve it in a huge, cut glass punch bowl for my big crew). Toss to mix. Serve immediately.

This salad disappears quickly every time I serve it. As with any recipe made with avocados, my family devours it—leaving me no leftovers to worry about.

-81-
Chicken Salad

I've hosted a lot of ladies brunches over the years, and have served chicken salad sandwiches at the majority of them. Every time I do, they get raving reviews.

The grapes and cranberries make it sweet, and the nuts and onions give it a nice crunch.

I always make a little more than I think I need, as it keeps well when refrigerated and tastes every bit as good the second time around.

> 2-3 cooked chicken breasts, cubed
> 2 cups of white grapes, cut in half
> 1 cup sliced almonds or coarsely chopped pecans
> ½ cup dried cranberries
> 1 bunch green onions, chopped
> 1½ cups mayonnaise or Miracle Whip
> freshly ground black pepper, to taste

Combine ingredients, mix thoroughly. Serve chilled on a bed of lettuce, with club crackers, or as filling in croissant or Hawaiian roll sandwiches. Anyway you serve it, it's delish.

Section 12: Rabbit Food

-82-
Black Bean Salad

This refrigerated salad really hits the spot in the heat of summer. It's popular enough with my kids that I usually have to double this recipe, and we still have no leftovers.

>1½ cups freshly cooked black beans (or a 15-oz can)
>1 can shoe peg corn (or 1½ cups frozen corn)
>1 small red onion, diced
>1 red bell pepper, seeded and chopped
>2 Tbsp fresh lime juice
>1 avocado, cut into chunks
>1 Tbsp olive oil
>1 small jalapeño pepper (optional)
>salt & pepper to taste
>1 cup fresh cilantro, chopped

Drain beans and corn. Mix with all the remaining ingredients except for cilantro, including seeded and minced jalapeño pepper (if desired).

Chill in the refrigerator until ready to eat. Top with chopped cilantro just before serving.

Section 13

The Main Event

Section 13: The Main Event

-83-
King Ranch Chicken

I make this dish the way I remember my mother making it during my childhood. I loved it then, and still love it now.

My husband has a bit of an aversion to casseroles, but we've found that he likes this dish, too, as long as I call it by a different name. Thus, for him, we've renamed it "stacked chicken enchiladas." Sometimes, I even go to the trouble of wrapping the filling in the tortillas for his sake, but either way, the basic recipe remains the same:

- 3 broiled chicken breasts, sliced thin
- 1 yellow onion, diced
- 1 can cream of chicken soup
- 1 can Rotel tomatoes
- 2 dozen soft corn tortillas
- 1-2 cups grated Colby jack cheese

Combine chicken, onion, and canned goods in a large mixing bowl. Tear the tortillas into small pieces and place them in the bottom of a greased 9×13 baking dish. Spread half the chicken mixture over this, then top with half the grated cheese. Repeat with another layer of tortillas, chicken mixture, and cheese. Bake in a 350° oven for 25-30 minutes or until cheese bubbles. Makes 8-12 servings.

Hint: Use any leftovers as a starting point for making tortilla soup (see recipe on page 107).

Sit Down & Eat

-84-
Easy Cheese Enchiladas

These enchiladas aren't fancy, but they're delicious. We take them with us to the pool in the summertime. Not your typical picnic fare, but they're fast and easy—I can have them ready to go in the time it takes the children to get into their swimsuits—with minimal mess.

>   non-stick cooking spray
>   corn tortillas
>   grated cheese (we usually use Colby-jack)
>   diced onions
>   1 can of chili (no beans)

Pre-heat oven to 350 degrees. Stack tortillas in a tortilla warmer after lightly spraying the top of each tortilla with cooking spray. Microwave on high for 3 minutes. In a 9×13 pan, sprinkle a little cheese and onions on two tortillas at a time, then quickly roll them up to form enchiladas. Be careful, those tortillas are steaming hot!

When you've rolled as many as your family can eat (we usually make two pans full—about 3 dozen), top with chili, sprinkle a little cheese and onion over that, and bake at 350 degrees for 10-15 minutes, or until cheese begins to bubble. Serve with tortilla chips, picante sauce, and a green salad.

Section 13: The Main Event

-85-
Mama's Meatloaf

This is a variation of the meatloaf my mother made when I was growing up, only she used cracker crumbs instead of oats and dried onion and garlic instead of fresh. Mine still tastes very old fashioned, especially when paired with mashed potatoes, whole kernel corn, and green beans.

- 2 lbs lean ground beef
- 1 small yellow onion, diced
- ¾ tsp salt
- ¾ tsp pepper
- 2 cloves garlic, minced
- ¾ cup ketchup
- 2 eggs
- 3 tsp Worcestershire sauce
- ¾ cup raw oats

Mix ingredients thoroughly (I just slip on a pair of surgical gloves and use my hands to knead it). Divide mixture and pat into two greased loaf pans. Bake at 350° F for one hour. Remove from oven and top with ketchup. Let sit for five minutes, then slice before serving.

I usually double this recipe and put the extra loaves, uncooked, in the freezer for another time. When we're ready to eat meatloaf again, I thaw them in the refrigerator overnight, then cook according to the directions above.

-86-
Spaghetti with Meat Sauce

My husband's all-time favorite dish is spaghetti. He likes it even better left over the second day, once the noodles have had time to soak in the flavor of all those herbs and spices in my marinara sauce.

Occasionally, I'll try to make this dish more healthful by substituting ground turkey or minced carrots and zucchini for the meat or whole wheat pasta or spaghetti squash for the noodles, but none of those versions satisfy him like the real deal, made with this tried and true recipe:

- 1 lb. of lean ground beef
- 1 yellow onion, diced
- 4-5 cloves fresh garlic, minced
- 1 can tomato sauce
- 1 can diced tomatoes
- 2 Tbsp Italian seasoning
- 1 small pkg. of spaghetti noodles

Brown ground beef and drain off the fat. Sauté garlic and onion until translucent and add to beef. Add tomatoes, sauce, and seasoning. Reduce and let simmer while cooking noodles according to directions on box. Serve meat sauce atop noodles with sides of garlic bread and tossed salad.

Section 13: The Main Event

-87-
Fiery Grilled Salmon

I was first introduced to this delicious recipe by my sister, who has always been an excellent cook and has a flair for making healthful dishes taste great.

> 1-2 lbs. salmon fillets or steaks
> ½ cup vegetable oil
> ¼ cup soy sauce
> ¼ cup balsamic vinegar
> ½ cup green onions, chopped
> 1 Tbsp brown sugar
> 2 cloves garlic, minced
> 1 ½ tsp ground ginger
> 2 tsp crushed red pepper flakes

Place salmon in a plastic bag. In a small bowl, combine all other ingredients. Pour over the fish, seal bag, and marinate in the refrigerator 4-6 hours.

Grill over medium heat until fish flakes easily with a fork (about ten minutes per inch of thickness). Cook with flesh side down for 6-7 minutes, then turn skin side down for the last 3-4. The skin will tend to stick to the grill, and it is an easy way to get the fish skinned before serving.

I really like salmon and frequently order it when we eat out, but I've yet to find a restaurant version that tastes better than this. The flavor is superb!

Sit Down & Eat

-88-
Crispy Tacos

About half of my kids are carnivores (like Dad), and the other half prefer a plant-based diet (like Mom).

Fortunately, that doesn't stop us from enjoying our weekly Taco Tuesdays. It still works, as long as we let everyone build their own. That way vegans can stick with beans and bell peppers while everybody else piles on beef and queso.

VEGAN OPTIONS:
- black beans
- rice
- refried beans
- shredded cabbage
- lettuce
- tomatoes
- pico de gallo
- avocados
- cilantro
- bright bell peppers

MEATIER CHOICES:
- ground beef
- spicy chicken
- shredded pork
- fajita steak
- grated cheddar
- crumbled goat cheese
- queso blanco

We let whatever's in the refrigerator at the time determine the number and variety of choices we offer, then serve it all with crispy taco shells or soft, warm tortillas (corn or flour). A generous helping of chips with salsa or guacamole on the side, and everyone's happy!

Section 13: The Main Event

-89-
Breaded & Baked Tilapia

One of the things I love most about this dish is that I can cook it in the oven without making the whole house smell fishy. I usually use tilapia, but any mild white fish, such as cod or orange roughy, is good prepared this way. This recipe yields nice, flakey fillets with a crispy brown crust. But they're baked, so you can enjoy them without all the extra fat used in frying.

- 3-4 white fish fillets
- ½ cup of flour, for dusting
- 2 eggs, beaten
- 1 cup seasoned bread crumbs
- 1 tsp garlic powder
- 2 Tbsp grated parmesan cheese
- ½ stick butter, melted
- 1 medium lemon

Preheat oven to 350° F. Beat eggs thoroughly; set aside. In another bowl, mix bread crumbs, parmesan cheese, and garlic. Cut fillets into 2-inch strips, then dredge in flour, dip in eggs, and roll in bread crumb mixture. Place on a non-stick cookie sheet. Repeat with remaining fillets, then drizzle butter over all before putting them in the oven. Bake in preheated oven for 15 minutes or until fish flakes with a fork. Serve with fresh lemon wedges.

Section 14

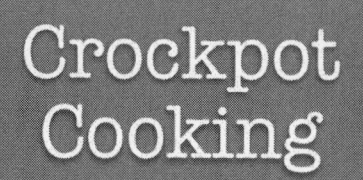

Crockpot Cooking

Section 14: Crockpot Cooking

-90-
Fix It and Forget It

The nice thing about cooking with a crockpot is that you can start a meal early in the day, even before the kids get up or the schedule gets busy, and not have to think about it again until it is time to eat. By then, the kitchen is filled with delectable smells that beckon everybody to gather at the table for dinner.

The trouble with cooking in a crockpot is that it takes so long, so unless you remember to start early, you'll have to come up with another plan for dinner. (That's where my new pressure cooker comes in handy, but that's another story for another day.)

Fortunately, recipes abound for making several batches of meals at once—two, four, even six weeks' worth—so that getting a fresh, hot meal to the dinner table each night takes even less brainwork. You can freeze a month's worth of crockpot meals in a single afternoon, then all you have to do is move it from freezer to fridge each night before bed, then slide it into your slow cooker the following morning.

One of my favorite recipe sources for this kind of cooking is New Leaf Wellness, because none of the ingredients need to be precooked before freezing. It's the simplest way I know of to prepare nutritious, delicious dishes for your family without slaving in the kitchen for hours every day.

-91-
Cranberry Chicken with Green Beans

The thing I love about this recipe is that it can be mixed up in advance, several batches at a time, and frozen until you're ready to cook it. There's no need to precook the chicken. Just thaw overnight, then slide it into your slow cooker the following morning.

I learned that trick from New Leaf Wellness, and you will find this and lots of other freezer meal recipes on their website. Every one we've tried have been super simple but scrumptious.

- 1 small onion, diced
- 1 can whole cranberry sauce
- 2 cloves garlic, minced
- 2 Tbsp honey
- 2 Tbsp balsamic vinegar
- 2 Tbsp extra virgin olive oil
- 1/4 tsp crushed red pepper flakes
- 1/4 tsp ground black pepper
- 2 lbs boneless, skinless chicken breasts
- 1 16-oz pkg of frozen, uncut green beans

Place all ingredients in slow cooker and cook on low heat setting for 4-6 hours. My kids are huge fans of green beans, and these have an amazing flavor we all love.

Section 14: Crockpot Cooking

-92-
Sunday Roast

As a child, I don't remember being particularly fond of pot roast, but—go figure—eating roast as an adult invariably brings to mind a flood of the fondest memories I can conjure up.

This is especially true when the meal is prepared the way my mother cooked it: fork tender, topped with onions and brown gravy, and flanked by a hearty helping of carrots and potatoes.

It works out well that I like it now as much as I do, because pot roast is one of the easiest meals there is. Mom made hers on the stovetop, but it's just as yummy (and even easier) to prepare it in a crockpot following these directions:

- 2-3 lb cut of boneless beef chuck roast
- 1 lb mini carrots
- 3-4 large russet potatoes, cut into chunks
- 1 yellow onion, sliced into rings
- 1 cup of water
- 1 pkg. Lipton onion soup mix
- 1 can of cream of mushroom soup

Combine all ingredients in a 6-qt crockpot and cook on low for 8 hours. Roast should be tender and shred easily.

-93-
Baked Apples

Get up early and put a batch of cinnamon apples in your crockpot, and your house will smell amazing by the time the rest of the family rises.

These baked apples are simple to make. You can even prepare them ahead of time and refrigerate them overnight in the stoneware insert. Drop it into the warming sleeve the following morning, and you're good to go!

6-7 Gala apples (cored)
¼ cup brown sugar
¼ cup walnuts, chopped
¼ cup raisins or dried cranberries
2 Tbsp butter (melted)
½ tsp cinnamon
¼ tsp nutmeg
1 cup orange juice

Mix sugar, nuts, raisins, butter and spices together, and pack mixture firmly into the hollow center of cored apples. Place stuffed apples in the bottom of a 6-qt. slow cooker. Pour orange juice over all, cover, and cook on low heat setting for 3-4 hours.

Section 14: Crockpot Cooking

-94-
Layered Lasagna

Spaghetti may be my husband's favorite (see p. 124), but his sons prefer lasagna. The sauce is similar for both, but I love the fact I can layer the lasagna into our crockpot and let it cook to perfection while I work on other projects.

- 1 lb. of lean ground beef
- 1 yellow onion, diced
- 4-5 cloves fresh garlic, minced
- 2 cans tomato sauce
- 2 Tbsp Italian seasoning
- 12 oz cottage cheese
- ½ cup parmesan cheese, shredded
- 1 lb. mozzarella cheese, shredded
- 1 Tbsp parsley
- 1 egg
- 12 oz lasagna noodles, uncooked

Brown beef, onion, and garlic in a frying pan. Add tomato sauce and Italian seasoning. Set aside ¼ cup of mozzarella. Mix remaining mozzarella with cottage cheese, parmesan cheese, and beaten egg. Layer lasagna into crockpot by spooning a layer of meat sauce in the bottom, topped with uncooked noodles, then cheese mixture, then more noodles, more sauce. Repeat. Sprinkle the reserved mozzarella over the last layer of meat sauce, then cook on low for 4-5 hours.

-95-
Pinto Beans with Ham

I was raised on beans and cornbread and still consider that pairing the full meal deal. To the meat lover I married, however, pinto beans were a side dish—and a superfluous one at that.

Fast forward 30 years, and my husband has become sold on the benefits of a plant-based diet—even if he isn't extremely disciplined about adopting one himself. Consequently, he's more willing than ever before to eat a couple of bowls of lentils or beans and call it dinner.

That's great, because beans are easy to cook (especially in a crock pot) and are easy on the pocketbook, as well. A ham bone makes them right tasty, but for a true vegan meal, you'll want to leave that ingredient out.

1 lb. dry pinto beans
8 cups water for cooking
1 ham bone (with a little meat still on it)
½ tsp salt

Pick beans and discard any rocks. Soak in cold crockpot overnight. Drain water in the morning, add remaining ingredients, and cook on high for 6-8 hours. Remove bone (but leave the little pieces of ham). Serve with cornbread and green onions. Beans, beans, good for your heart….

Section 14: Crockpot Cooking

-96-
Turkey & Cheese Melts

This is not a dish most people would think about cooking in a crockpot, but when my husband bought a new van several years ago, and I realized it had a three-pronged outlet in the front seat, I decided to take full advantage of it on our next road trip.

I plugged our slow cooker in and let our meals cook while we traveled, then served them up at rest stops along the way. It was much more economical than springing for snacks and drinks at the gas station or stopping at restaurants every time someone started to feel hungry.

We tried several different recipes during that first road trip, but the turkey and cheese melts were by far the easiest and least messy. I'd line Dad and the kids up by the van in the hotel parking lot with a square of foil and a split dinner roll in each hand, then go down the row spreading spicy mustard, then layering on piles of shaved turkey and thick slabs of cheddar before wrapping each sandwich and marking the foil with each family member's initials, then stacking them in the crockpot and setting it on "warm."

Two or three hours down the road, we'd pull over at a rest stop and slam them down with bottled water. Good stuff... and very satisfying!

Section 15

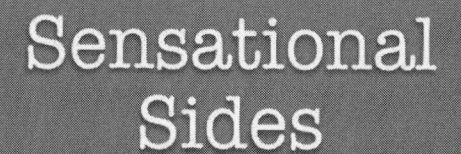

Sensational Sides

Section 15: Sensational Sides

-97-
Sweet Potato Fries

We used to fry our potatoes with onions, drain them on a paper towel, and eat them while they were still piping hot. The healthier version below is baked, not fried, and packed with all the vitamins and nutrients so plentiful in sweet potatoes. Plus, they are absolutely delicious (and not as heavy as the pan fried variety).

olive oil (for tossing)
5 sweet potatoes, peeled and cut into ¼-inch strips
1 Tbsp seasoning salt (recipe follows)
½ tsp paprika
1 cup salt
¼ cup black pepper
¼ cup garlic powder

Preheat oven to 450°F. Grease cookie sheet. In a large bowl, toss sweet potatoes with just enough oil to coat. Sprinkle with seasoning salt and paprika. Mix well, then spread sweet potatoes in single layer on prepared baking sheet (for best results, don't overcrowd). Bake 20-30 minutes, turning occasionally, until sweet potatoes are tender and golden brown. Cool 5-10 minutes before serving.

Excess seasoning salt may be stored up to six months in an airtight container to use next time (these fries are addictive, so you'll probably be making another batch soon).

Sit Down & Eat

-98-
Green Bean Casserole

A longtime standard at family gatherings and church potlucks, green bean casserole is still a favorite for most of our kids. Even though I normally double the recipe, it's always the first side dish finished at our Thanksgiving and Christmas dinners.

This is the recipe my mom always used. I know the cream of mushroom soup and fried onions are frowned upon in this health-conscious age, but eating this casserole once or twice a year can't hurt us too much. After all, it's a tradition!

> 2 cans green beans
> 1 can cream of mushroom soup
> ¼ cup milk
> ground black pepper (to taste)
> 2 cups French-fried onions

Preheat oven to 350° F. Combine beans, soup, milk, pepper, and half the onions in a 9x13 inch glass baking dish.

Bake 20 minutes or until bubbly. Remove from oven. Top with remaining onions. Bake for 5 more minutes. Serve warm.

Section 15: Sensational Sides

-99-
Parmesan-Crusted Asparagus Spears

My daughter Rebekah introduced us to this fabulous dish. Serve them as a side, an appetizer, or maybe just for an afternoon snack. They're good anytime!

> 2 lbs fresh asparagus spears (approx. ½-inch thick)
> ½ tsp salt
> ground black pepper (to taste)
> 1 cup flour
> 2 eggs
> 1½ cups grated parmesan
> ¾ cup seasoned bread crumbs
> 1/8 tsp cayenne pepper

Preheat oven to 450°F. Poke holes in asparagus stalks with a fork. Sprinkle it with salt and pepper and set aside.

Combine 1 cup of the parmesan with the bread crumbs and cayenne pepper in a shallow bowl. Beat eggs in a separate bowl. Put flour alone in third bowl. Dredge each asparagus spear first in flour, then egg, then bread crumb mixture. Place in single layer on foil lined baking sheet. Bake on center rack 6-8 minutes or until just beginning to brown. Sprinkle with reserved parmesan, return to oven for 6-8 minutes longer. Transfer to platter and serve warm.

-100-
Spicy Beet Fries

We got hooked on beets at a local Asian restaurant. Even our kids love this lightly fried version and would often make an entire meal out of them. Sadly, the restaurant eventually closed down, but not before the chef shared his secret for making this delectable side dish:

> 5 large beets
> 1 Tbsp oil + more for frying
> 1 Tbsp vinegar
> ½ cup cornstarch
> ½ cup Kewpie (Japanese mayonnaise)
> shichimi togarashi (Japanese 7 spice blend)
> 2 Tbsp sliced green onions

Place beets in center of large sheet of foil. Drizzle with oil and vinegar. Cover with more foil, crimping edges tightly. Roast in 375° oven for 2 hours.

Remove roasted beets from oven and slide them out of their skins. Cut into 1-inch cubes. Chill in refrigerator.

To fry, heat a small amount of oil in a frying pan. Toss beets with cornstarch, and lightly fry in oil, 2½ cups at a time. Serve with a side of mayonnaise for dipping. Garnish with shichimi togarashi and green onions.

Section 15: Sensational Sides

-101-
Roasted Brussels Sprouts

I know, I know. Everybody hates Brussels sprouts—especially kids. Right? Well, after you try this recipe, you may learn to love America's most hated vegetable as much as our family does. In fact, my ten-year-old was reading over my shoulder as I typed this chapter. "Those are so good," he said, unsolicited. "Can we eat them again soon?"

The recipe is simple. First, set your oven to 350 degrees. Next, wash your sprouts. Be sure to use cold water when you rinse these little guys—Brussels sprouts don't smell very pretty when they're raw, and if you rinse with hot water, your family may sniff the air and accuse one another of passing gas! The good news is that once they're roasted, Brussels spouts smell almost as good as they taste.

After rinsing Brussels sprouts, cut a thin layer off the stem end of each one, then slice into halves. Drizzle sprouts with olive oil, then sprinkle to taste with salt, pepper, and paprika. Pop into a warm (350°F) oven. Roast for 20 to 30 minutes.

When the sprouts are finished, they're fork-tender and delicious. Our kids routinely polish off several pounds in a single sitting. They're irresistible!

Section 16

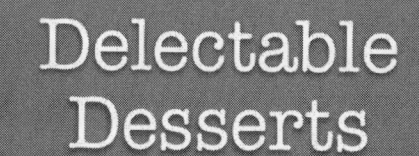

Delectable Desserts

Section 16: Delectable Desserts

-102-
Chocolate Delight

For years, my father had my mom convinced this dessert was no good the second day…. Not true! That was just Dad's excuse for polishing it all off before bedtime.☺

- 1 cup flour
- ¼ cup powdered sugar
- 1 cup chopped pecans
- ½ cup margarine
- 1 (8-oz) pkg of cream cheese
- 1 cup powdered sugar
- 1 cup Cool Whip
- 1 (4-oz) pkg instant chocolate pudding mix
- 1 (4-oz) pkg instant vanilla pudding mix
- 4 cups milk
- ½ cup of slivered almonds, toasted

Preheat oven to 350°F. Let margarine and cream cheese soften to room temperature. Mix flour, ¼ cup powdered sugar, chopped pecans, and margarine together. Press into a baking dish and bake for 20 minutes. Cool thoroughly.

Mix together cream cheese, 1 cup powdered sugar, and cool whip. Spread mixture on cooled crust, set aside. Mix chocolate and vanilla instant pudding with milk. Carefully spread a layer of this mixture on top of cream cheese layer without mixing the two. Top with a final layer of cool whip (as much as you want). Sprinkle with slivered, toasted almonds before serving. Refrigerate leftovers (*if any* ☺).

-103-
Blackberry Crumble

Our family has been fortunate enough to have a wild blackberry thicket growing near just about every house we've ever lived in. We love hunting the berries together every spring. They ripen right about the time that our son Isaac celebrates his birthday, and he usually requests I make him a crumble instead of a birthday cake. Here's the recipe I use:

- 2 sticks real cream butter
- 2¼ cups flour
- ¾ cup brown sugar (packed)
- ¾ cup granulated sugar
- ½ tsp salt
- ¾ cup rolled oats
- 2½ cups blackberries (blueberries will work, too)

Preheat oven to 375°F. Butter and spread berries in the bottom of a 9" x 13" glass baking dish.

In separate large bowl, whisk together dry ingredients. Cut cold butter in using a pastry blender until large clumps form. Using a rubber spatula, gently mix in oats. Crumble this mixture over the top of the berries, covering the fruit as evenly as possible.

Bake 45-50 minutes, until juices are bubbling and topping is browned. Serve warm with a scoop of vanilla ice cream.

Section 16: Delectable Desserts

-104-
Peanut Butter Cookies

Want an easy recipe to get your kids excited about cooking? This one has consistently done that job in our family.

Peanut butter cookies are one of the first things our children learn to cook. A little success with these builds their confidence, then soon they're ready to tackle much more complicated recipes.

>   1 cup peanut butter
>   1 cup sugar
>   1 egg

Just these three ingredients, and that's it! Cream them together. Drop by rounded teaspoon on a cookie sheet. Flatten with a fork. Bake at 350° for 10-11 minutes.

Let them cool a bit before removing from the pan.

This recipe makes about three dozen small cookies or one dozen large ones (provided they don't eat too much of the dough—one of our boys ate more of them raw than baked when he used to make them).

-105-
Rice Crispy Treats

Here's another quick and easy three-ingredient recipe. My daughter learned to make these at a friend's house, then came straight home and got the rest of our family hooked on them.

> 1 stick of butter
> 1 10.5-oz pkg of mini-marshmallows
> 6 cups crispy rice cereal

Melt butter and marshmallows over medium-high heat, stirring constantly, until mixture is smooth and begins to bubble. Remove from heat, stir in cereal, pour into 9 inch x 13 inch pan (spray first with cooking spray), and pat it down smoothly (it's less messy if you'll spray your hand with cooking spray before attempting this step. We use disposable, food-service gloves, which we also spray liberally with cooking spray).

Let treats cool, then cut into squares. Yum-yum. For all you chocolate lovers, these are also very good made with Cocoa Crispies cereal.

Alternatively, you can add ½ cup of peanut butter to the butter and marshmallow cream mixture, add an extra cup of rice crispies, and top the bars with melted chocolate chips. They're really good that way, too. ☺

Section 16: Delectable Desserts

-106-
No-Bake Chocolate Cookies

Once upon a time, elementary school cafeterias included desserts with student lunches. I'm not sure that's even allowed these days, but for kids who may be missing out, here's a recipe for the best dessert my own lunchroom ladies ever offered. Forty years later, it still a personal favorite:

½ cup butter
2 cups sugar
½ cup milk
4 Tbsp cocoa
Pinch of salt
½ cup peanut butter
2 tsp vanilla
3 cups rolled oats

Combine butter, sugar, milk, cocoa and salt in a 4-qt saucepan. Bring to a rolling boil over medium heat, then cook for 1 minute longer.

Remove from heat and stir in peanut butter until melted. Add vanilla, then mix in oats. Drop by heaping tablespoons onto wax paper. Cool completely before serving.

Section 17

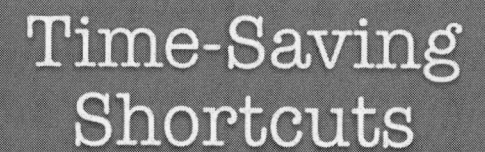

Time-Saving Shortcuts

Section 17: Time-Saving Shortcuts

-107-
Perfect Pasta

I don't know if you've ever tried eating overcooked pasta, but it is sticky and gooey and gross. Unfortunately, I've cooked my fair share of it over the years, primarily because I tend to get called away or otherwise distracted in the middle of food preparations and end up boiling my pasta for much longer than the package recommends.

At least, that's how it worked until I discovered the following trick for preparing perfect pasta, every time:

Bring salted water to a rapid boil. Add pasta. Replace the lid and remove from heat. Let pasta sit, covered, for a minimum of 15 minutes before serving.

And that's it.

If you get called away and forget it, or if it takes a little more than 15 minutes to get the rest of dinner ready, no worries. It won't burn or scorch or boil off all the water or turn mushy and gross in any way. The pasta is cooked to perfection, every time.

When you are ready to serve it, simply drain the water, add oil or sauce, and dig in!

Sit Down & Eat

-108-
Big Batch Cooking

I know a lot of ladies who prepare a whole month's worth of meals in a single afternoon. I admire their efficiency, but big batch cooking looks a little different at our house. When feeding as big a crew as we have, every meal means cooking in bulk. Even so, I often make double the amount of ground beef or beans or bread dough I need for the dish I'm preparing, as doing so saves time in the long run.

That way, if I'm using any of those ingredients later in the week, I'll be one step closer to completing the meal than if I had to start again from scratch. Here are some of the ways preparing double the amount of certain ingredients plays out in my kitchen:

- ground beef: you can use half of it for tacos one night and the other half to make spaghetti the next
- baked potatoes: serve half of them fully loaded for dinner and use the rest in potato soup or potato salad later in the week
- beans: enjoy half the pot with a pan of cornbread, then mash and refry the rest to use later in burritos
- boiled eggs: boil a big batch, then serve some of them halved and deviled, some sliced on salads, then peel and eat the extras plain for a protein-rich snack.

Section 17: Time-Saving Shortcuts

-109-
Freezer Meals

Stocking the freezer with crockpot meals and casseroles is a great way to save time. With the right recipes (I love the ones by *New Leaf Wellness*), you can knock out 6-8 meals in about 15 minutes.

It's a little harder to stock the freezer ahead of time now that half our family has gone vegan. Fresh, raw fruits and veggies are the basis of most of our meals these days, but the freezer can still help cut prep time for some dishes:

- When our bananas start to get overripe, we slice them up and freeze them in Ziploc bags to use in fruit smoothies. We do the same with fresh strawberries, blueberries, and mangos. If you're really ambitious, you can do as my daughter does and combine all the fruits you need for different smoothie recipes in single serve portions, so that all you need to do is empty the bag in the blender and add a little almond milk.
- Lots of our favorite soups freeze well—lentil, tomato, minestrone—so I'll often cook a double batch, eat half, and freeze the rest for another night.
- Homemade pizza dough freezes well, as do most of our favorite toppings (onions, mushrooms, bell peppers). Then it's just a matter of thawing the dough and topping it with sauce and veggies before baking. Easy cheesy!

-110-
How to Boil an Egg

As I mentioned earlier, I barely knew how to boil water when I left home. Luckily for me, there are a lot of handy things you can do with boiling water. You can brew tea, make cocoa, cook pasta, steam rice, stew potatoes, and boil eggs—just to mention a few.

For perfectly hard boiled eggs every time, try the trick my mother taught me:

Place 1-4 eggs into a 2-quart sauce pan and cover with water. Put the pan on the stove top and turn the burner to the highest heat setting, then set a timer for exactly 15 minutes.

When the timer goes off, turn the burner off, take the pan of the stove, and immediately immerse the eggs in ice cold water. Cooling them off quickly will prevent the yolks from turning gray.

When the eggs have sufficiently cooled for easy handling, peel off the shells. Then they are ready to be halved and deviled or sliced for a chef salad or chopped for an egg sandwich… or eaten whole with a little salt and pepper.

Enjoy!

Section 17: Time-Saving Shortcuts

-111-
Grocery Shopping

I was so excited when my children were old enough to send to the store with a list, so they could do my grocery shopping for me. Until then, I'd have my oldest push a cartload of his siblings while I pushed the cart of groceries up and down each aisle collecting what we needed and fielding incessant requests for stuff we didn't.

Lately, I've been doing my grocery shopping online using Walmart's Pick Up service. What a blessing! If that's not an option in your neighborhood, the following tips will make the grocery shopping easier, no matter who's doing it:

- shop from a list—you're far less likely to blow your budget if you get only the items you went after
- shop when you're full—it's easier to avoid impulse purchases when you aren't famished
- group your selections—to simplify shopping trips, divide your list into categories: canned goods, dairy case items, produce, frozen foods, etc.
- linger in the produce section—pound-for-pound, they're often less expensive, more filling, and more healthful than most of the highly-processed stuff
- make exceptions—if you find a slashed price on something you'll use, stock up on as much as you can polish off before it expires

- AFTERWORD -

Well, that brings us to the end of the book! I hope what you've read has motivated you to make your family mealtimes more memorable—or at least to prioritize eating together as often as possible, for as fun as occasional theme nights and mood music and special holiday dinners can be, they make a poor substitute for consistently gathering around the table together to break bread and share thoughts.

Sitting down on a daily basis to at least one simple meal prepared in love for (or *with!*) your children, discussing the days' events, spending time together—that's what our families are really hungry for, whether they realize it or not.

So take what you've gleaned from *Sit Down & Eat* and give the ideas that resonate with your family's circumstances, goals, and personalities a try. If you incorporate just one of these suggestions into your schedule per week, you'll find enough ideas here to keep you busy for two full years!

That's enough time to establish lasting lifestyle changes and healthier mealtime routines—all while making some fabulous memories that you and your children will treasure for years to come!

May God's richest blessings be yours,

Jennifer Flanders

www.flandersfamily.info
www.facebook.com/TheFlandersFamily

- Coming Soon -
from Prescott Publishing

PACK UP & LEAVE

Fun Ideas for Traveling with Children

Jennifer Flanders

- MORE BOOKS -
by Jennifer Flanders

*25 Ways to Communicate Respect
to Your Husband: A Handbook for Wives*

*Balance: The Art of Minding
What Matters Most*

*Count Your Blessings:
A Devotional Journal for Thanksgiving*

*Get Up & Go: Fun Ideas
for Getting Fit as a Family*

*Glad Tidings: The First 25 Years
of Flanders Family Christmas Letters*

*Love Your Husband/ Love Yourself:
Embracing God's Purpose
for Passion in Marriage*

*Sweet Child of Mine:
A Devotional Journal for Mothers*

- OTHER TITLES -
from Prescott Publishing

25 Ways to Show Love to Your Wife:
A Handbook for Husbands
by Doug Flanders, MD

How to Encourage Your Husband:
Ideas to Revitalize Your Marriage
by Nancy Campbell

How to Encourage Your Children:
Tools to Help You Raise Mighty Warriors for God
by Nancy Campbell

Life's Big Questions
Colossians
by Doug Flanders, MD

The Sweet Gospel:
13 Weeks of Savoring the Good News
by Mandy Ballard

Made in the USA
Las Vegas, NV
09 November 2021